Change Your Habits, Change Your Life

Celebrating
30 Years of Publishing
in India

Praise for *Change Your Habits, Change Your Life*

'Written from the heart, this book contains wisdom that one needs to transform their life. Ashdin is someone who I know will not preach to the choir. The exercises mentioned in the book are reflective and easy. I loved the minute details from Ashdin's life strewn across the chapters that show change is possible through habits. The thread of imagination, determination and zest for life is constant throughout the book. The simple and effective read is your first step towards leading the life you've admired in others. Thank you for making success and joy attainable for everyone!'

—Kubbra Sait

Praise for The Habit Coach™

'Working with Ashdin has been the best investment I have made. He transformed my life by supporting me in building micro habits that have led to an overall lifestyle change.'

—Talia Ahmed

'What's the toughest part about habits? No, it's not building it. It's keeping at it. Ashdin not only helps you build habits but also teaches you to maintain them. He is your one-stop-shop for the Hows and Whys of all things "habit"!'

—Neha A. Jacob, founder, Purple Sage

'Ashdin brought a clear understanding of what my stress triggers were and how they affected my food and sleep patterns … Ashdin's intelligence, wit, articulateness and patience shine forth in the way he coaches. He makes picking up new habits and stacking habits easy!'

—Avani Patel

'While working with Ashdin, The Habit Coach™, I've achieved a much-needed balance in my otherwise meaningless and confusing life. I have revived my withering relationships.'

—Radhika Gupta

'Ashdin explains things in detail and gives options that can be sustained for the long term. I advise everyone to take this journey to be their superior version; and with someone like Ashdin as your wingman, the ride will be Awesome.'

—Jay Sagar

'Ashdin's first assignment for me was to visualize my ideal life in five years. His instruction—go wild! And I did. Now, I periodically review my personal and professional aspirations. The reflection helps me course correct. Another Ashdin insight—focus your energy on the present day, not on time. I thought about what gives me energy and what drains it—people, work and food. This helped me set a better daily routine—a habit that transformed my day!'

—Sanjay Jindal, managing director,
Western Heat and Forge

Change Your Habits, Change Your Life

YOUR GUIDE TO AN AWESOME LIFE

ASHDIN DOCTOR

HarperCollins *Publishers* India

First published in India by HarperCollins *Publishers* 2023
4th Floor, Tower A, Building No. 10, DLF Cyber City,
DLF Phase II, Gurugram, Haryana – 122002
www.harpercollins.co.in

2 4 6 8 10 9 7 5 3 1

P-ISBN: 978-93-5629-538-4
E-ISBN: 978-93-5629-539-1

The views and opinions expressed in this book are the author's own and the facts are as reported by him, and the publishers are not in any way liable for the same.

None of the content in this book is intended to be a substitute for professional medical advice and should not be relied on as health or medical advice, diagnosis or treatment. Always seek the guidance of your doctor or other qualified health professional with any questions you may have regarding your health or a medical condition.

The names, ages and other identifying details about clients have been changed to protect their privacy.

Typeset in 11.5/15 Adobe Caslon Pro at
Manipal Technologies Limited, Manipal

Printed and bound at
Thomson Press (India) Ltd

Dedicated to my first habit teachers—my parents, Villy and Vispy Doctor. They have always supported me in all the crazy habits that I have explored over the years—habits that I now teach, share and coach.

Dedicated to all my beloved coachees. Their trust and faith in me have made this book possible. I grew with them as much as they grew with me.

And finally dedicated to you, the reader. Thank you for investing in this book. Please make it a habit to read it every day. You may even re-read this book every year to remind yourself of habits that you continue to form and evolve.

Contents

Introduction

The Trigger That Changed My Life

The shirt I had put on moments ago, had turned into a damp mess. I could feel my heart pounding, as though desperately trying to break free. My fingers were getting cold and were shaking. I took off the shirt and wore another. Sweat was now dripping down my face and body. I tried to ignore it, as I was in a hurry and already late for work. My chest was clenching tighter and tighter and I began to gasp; it was now difficult to take in a single breath. All of a sudden my feet buckled under me and I found myself on the floor panting, clutching my chest and soaking wet. I had no idea what was happening to me. Was it a heart attack? Was it a panic attack? What could this have been?

The world around me spun and went dark. This was in May 2014.

Let's see how I got there.

I was born into a family of serial entrepreneurs. My parents had started our family business, Ormax Consultants Pvt. Ltd., a year after I was born. I grew up with the mindset that I would one day be running it. It was one of the leading qualitative market research companies. Family friends included managing directors of companies, owners of huge businesses, and other high achievers in their chosen fields. They became my role models. Our dinner table conversations revolved around marketing plans and five-year business projections. There was no doubt in my mind that I was going to join my family business. And I was excited to do it!

I joined Ormax straight out of college aged twenty as the company's youngest and most junior employee. I often joked that the only thing I outranked was the water cooler. Often, when you grow up in a family of such amazing high achievers, you tend to grow up with a chip on your shoulder and mine was my need to prove myself. I had to be the best at what I was doing and better than everyone else.

Shortly after joining—to prove myself—I enrolled in a part-time three-year MBA course. Understandably, my routine was hectic. Monday through Saturday I woke up at 6.30 a.m., reached the gym by 7 a.m., attended office from 9 a.m. to 5 p.m., and MBA classes from 6 p.m. to 9 p.m. Grit and determination had been woven into my daily ethos from an early age to the point that the harder something was, the more I wanted to do it. It had to be huge (and difficult) to be worthy enough.

I hadn't a clue that I was looking to prove myself and yearning for validation from everyone around me. Meanwhile my family was very conscious that no favouritism be shown to me at work. I found myself dealing with the constant push and pull of proving myself to the employees, most of whom knew me since my school days. To stop them seeing me as kid, I felt compelled to prove myself as a professional. Slowly and gradually all this started building up pressure and soon I was stressed all the time.

Clearly, as I can now see, I was compensating for a lack of something, maybe self-esteem. The trigger lay way back—when I was just finishing college, a family friend had sat me down and shared some home truths that had stung deep, and now my goal was to prove him wrong. 'Ashdin,' the friend had said, 'you are completely useless, you spend all day playing games, everything you have is because of your parents. Do you think you deserve any of this?'

And so, after slogging hard in my twenties and completing my MBA, I had finally been able to start my own division within the business at thirty. It was my first baby. And it obviously *had* to be the fastest-growing division! There was just no other option. Plus it *had* to be created completely by me and I could not ask for help from anyone else. Every single client was new, companies that our business had not approached before.

My twenties had been spent overloading my plate—working, studying, and striving to be seen as a sterling professional. In my thirties, my MBA done, I loaded my plate anew with new client acquisitions, project deliveries, the need to maintain my division's profitability, creating a team, marketing, creating new products; the list just seemed endless. In the rat race, to prove myself, I was creating a lot of stress for myself. And I refused to show weakness and ask for help.

By this time I was also married and things were not so rosy at home. My marriage was falling apart. We fought every night. As a result, there was no safe space or respite from either work stress or home stress. At least work made me feel like I was doing something meaningful and became an escape from home.

Instead of managing my stress, I started taking pride in telling people how stressed I was, how stressful things were. It slowly became my guilty pleasure and an escape from my present situation. You might have a similar guilty pleasure. This is because feeling stressed can make us feel we are doing something important.

Mental and emotional stress started affecting my body as I started stress eating. By thirty-one I weighed around 90 kilos, which is 18 kilos more than my ideal weight. My old gymming habit had been replaced with a nice big tummy. Anytime someone told me to lose weight, I would pat my tummy and say, 'It's a sign of prosperity.' I dismissed the thought that anything was wrong with my body. I had enough money to eat whatever I wanted, drink as much as I wanted, and oh! those desserts. I could just replace every meal with them.

Food was my escape from my world of stress and exhaustion. I took great pride in being able to eat more than anyone else and faster than anyone else. It filled a void. Friends and family started commenting how pudgy and dull my face looked. An aunt even commented on how my eyes lacked vibrancy and asked, 'Where is my old Ashdin?'

Their questions, or rather concern, made me angry. How dare they say something like this! Was I not hiding it well enough? No one knew what I was going through at home or at work, but I did say often that things were stressful, life was stressful. Yet, despite all of this, I believed I was healthy! I was doing all the right things to remain healthy, or so I believed.

I would wake up and eat a big bowl of cornflakes. On days I wanted to be super healthy it was granola. Both were drowned in a ton of milk and heaped with spoons of sugar for some added crunch. Hell, I deserved the sugar after making such a healthy choice! This would be followed by a tall glass-and-a-half of juice. Orange or a mixed-vegetable juice. The carton said no sugar added, so it must be healthy, right?

I slept for about four to five hours a night. Wasn't sleep just a waste of time? 'I will sleep when I am dead,' I used to say; who knew I was already so close to it! I watched TV till I couldn't keep my eyes open, till my mind had no more energy to register what was going on and hence became quiet. To be honest I did not know what a good night's sleep was. I had no idea what it felt like, to sleep and wake up rested. And since I had no idea what restful sleep felt like, I did not know what I was missing.

Sounds familiar?

Exercising had become an alien concept. Gymming was part of student life, when I was in college and even while doing my MBA. However, since then, the thought of exercise seemed strange. An adult and going to the gym? You must be crazy, who has time for that!

I thought exercise was such a useless waste of energy, and energy was already in short supply. I wasn't about to waste any on a silly treadmill. As for the treadmill at home, it was designed for one thing and one thing only, to hang my clothes on. Walking was another casualty, in fact it was unthinkable. I drove or took a rickshaw to the corner store. I mean, only mad people walked, why walk when you can roll. Right? It came to a point that I panted after climbing three flights of stairs at a normal or slower than normal pace. There was no chance of me doing a push-up. Hanging from a bar was close to impossible.

At the ripe old age of thirty-one, I had a backache or a headache every single day. I was just always in pain. I believed that everyone had backaches and one bought a massaging chair for them. It had come to a point where I believed the pain was normal and didn't bother discussing it with anyone. The idea of solving the root cause of these aches and pains did not even enter my mind. The rare occasion when I did not have a backache was a brief respite and cause for celebration. I still didn't believe anything was wrong with me or with my health, at least physically.

As for my mental stress, neither did I see it, nor did my family or friends! I did not take the pains as a warning sign. Nor did it occur to me that they could be caused by my daily habits. Instead, I believed that they were part of growing up and growing old! As long as I was crushing it at work, giving my all to my new division, earning lots of money and proving myself to everyone around me, I thought I was being successful. Eating in fancy restaurants and driving a good car. What more did I need from life?

To get back to that fateful day in May 2014, when I was getting ready for a meeting—I had spent the previous few days working on an important presentation and had maybe had a total of four hours of sleep over the last two days. As always, things were in a rush. Oh, the joy of that 'last-minute panic', the adrenaline rush! It's crazy how we always wait for the last minute to finish anything (this too is a habit)! On that fateful day when my body broke down and I lay unconscious on the floor, I was incredibly lucky because I regained consciousness after a few minutes and got back on my feet.

What would have been a warning sign for most induced a rather odd reaction. Part of me was obviously afraid that I might have had a heart attack at thirty-one, but part of me felt strangely proud to have survived. I congratulated myself saying, 'Look at you, good job, you worked so hard that you collapsed.' And so I got dressed and went to the meeting. No one was at home and I didn't tell anyone about this either.

However, after the meeting I realized I'd hit a turning point. Deep down I knew that something needed to change. I did not want to die at the age of thirty-one. I also had an epiphany. Had I died and had God asked me what I thought of this beautiful gift of His, my life, what would I say?

Would I say it was so-so, okay-okay, meh? That's when I decided that when I die, I want to say that I lived an awesome life.

A few days after this incident I looked at myself in the mirror and (finally) realized I did not like what I saw—the puffy face and eyes, my big belly, nor how old I looked. I didn't recognize the person in front of me. Have you ever felt that? It's a scary thing!

I decided to give myself the hardest possible goal that I could think of. That would be getting a six-pack. What could possibly be harder than that, right? As with everything else, I threw myself into this wholeheartedly too.

The next few months were spent trying every single workout programme I could think of. Jillian Michaels six-week six-pack (spoiler alert: it takes way more than six weeks). I went on to try P90x and Insanity and anything that promised me the body that I was lusting after. Each workout was gruelling. Remember this body hadn't moved in a while. I had a gym membership, but hadn't been in even once. I could not hang from a bar; my grip strength was non-existent. Come to think of it, it's a wonder how I managed to open jars of jam back then.

Then I discovered these things called seven-minute scientific workout, and Tabata four-minute workout. No longer did I have to be overwhelmed by long hardcore programmes and thirty- or sixty-minute-long workouts. All I needed was seven-minutes. Now that was doable. Or was it? I found I couldn't do a single push-up. If I went down, I stayed down. A plank or a wall sit was close to impossible.

But something strange started to happen as the weeks turned into months and the months piled on. The exercises began to get easier. I was able to do a push-up! And the day I got my first pull-up. Oh God! It was as if I had conquered the world! I felt invincible. It was that consistency of carrying on and not giving up that changed my body. Making exercise a habit, made me stronger and more able. Seeing progress, fuelled me onwards to grow and try harder things.

I soon realized that just exercise and crunches were not enough. We have been sold on this myth, that exercise is the only way to lose weight; my next deep dive was into nutrition and I tried every diet known to man (at the time). Low carb. Low fat. Atkins. GM. I was willing to try anything!

Each of these diets was so hard and it was difficult to maintain them—I could grit my teeth and get through a week or two, but there was no way to sustain them for the rest of my life. It was just too hard and so I began to yo-yo. Lose a few kilos and then gain a few kilos. Again nothing seemed to be working.

I felt like I had been lied to! Because I was doing what the magazines, websites and fitness gurus were saying, but nothing was truly changing. It was hard and frustrating.

The turning point in my journey came when I had three critical realizations: get your sources right; get a strong reason to change; and be long-term focused. Here's the way I understood these three.

Get your sources right: The source of one's knowledge was very important. Learn from science, not from common knowledge. How often are we guided on weight loss by a relative/friend/colleague who is clearly obese? Information that is often justified by saying 'people say XYZ is good for weight loss'. We must learn to question, who are these 'people'? Where is the science? Are they an authority in the field or not? Often it is something they have read in a magazine somewhere, but really know nothing much about.

Creating a habit based on bad information will create a habit that does not give results. It is a waste.

Remember getting and giving advice is easy, but finding the right advice is hard. Always question the source and get your sources right. I turned to books, reading lots and lots of them, and Podcasts were another big source of authentic knowledge.

Get a strong reason to change: Making a change in one's life has to come from a deep-seated place; emerging from an emotion or a desire that is very personal and unique to you. The stronger the desire and the deeper the emotional connection, the better the chance of you sticking to it. Very often we live in a superficial state of desires. We want things because others want them too. Or because others expect it from us. This is a clear path to failure. We need to understand just how deep our desires go. Are they just surface-level and fleeting? Or deep and emotional?

For me, my deep-seated desire was initially to get a six-pack, because I felt that the process to getting it would teach me all I had to know about getting fit. But once I had the six-pack, my single-pointed desire was to never be scared of my body again! My body should be able to do whatever I needed of it. Without fear.

Be long-term focused: Rapid and short-term changes do not work for long-term goals. We keep making short-term action plans for a goal that is long-term. If we have a long-term goal, we must have a long-term plan. A plan that can help build consistency. And nothing builds consistency like a habit. Focusing on what you do every day is the only way to consistency.

Once I realized this, I focused on things that I could be consistent with. Places where I could show up every day and make those small changes. Small changes that became my new habits.

I slowly changed the way I ate, exercised, slept, and de-stressed. Within a year, at thirty-two, I had my six-pack. But that was no longer the point, my goal and desire had changed to sustaining this change! For the first time in a long while my eyes were bright and filled with energy, even my skin tone had changed, there was a suppleness to it. I looked like I had aged backward!

The funny thing is that when I began this process of change, people delighted in making fun of me, making me feel like an outcast, or implying I was doing something silly. Later, it was the same people sought me out to ask how I managed it, because they had tried many times and failed.

Post success, friends would come up at parties or weddings and want to know all about it, 'Tell me how you did it? Give me a few tips!' But within a couple of minutes they would admit defeat, 'I don't think I have your self-discipline or your motivation' or 'I don't think I can do what you do'. That was a bit of a shock; I realized that people didn't start because: (i) they believed that they didn't have the self-discipline or motivation to successfully finish; and (ii) many had tried in the past and failed. That memory of failing prevented them from starting again!

If they were too scared to start, believed they lacked the willpower to see it through, lacked the motivation to remain consistent, how would any change ever take place? Half the battle, therefore, lay in 'just starting'. They needed to relearn the way they thought about change, because:

Fear of change + lack of motivation = No action

Having gone through my own personal transformation journey, I wanted to shout about it from the rooftops. I wanted to tell everybody just how easy it could be to change one's life, get healthier, fitter and calmer.

Every time I saw someone eating packaged or junk food, I wanted to grab their shoulders and a give them a good shake! I wanted to open people's eyes to the fact that they did not have to keep suffering the way they were. Knee problems, backaches, sleep issues and bloating etc., I wanted to show them how easy and practical it was to change one's life. And that's just what I did.

Launching Awesome180 and The Habit Coach™

We seek out change because we want to improve ourselves. We want our lives to get better. We want our relationships to improve. We want to see a change in our bank balance and watch it grow. We want to see a change in our health and our bodies. However, many of us are trapped in our comfort zone and fear of stepping out of it keeps us doing the same thing over and over again, while wishing things would change.

Our lives are nothing but an outcome of the daily choices we make. Most of these are made subconsciously in an unaware state and when repeatedly made, become our daily habits. My own personal efforts at transformation succeeded only when I realized that habits *could* generate change. This was a big enough deal for me to pause working at the family business, so that I could create solutions for those frustrated with their lives but unable to turn things around! And so in 2017, I launched a programme called Awesome180 where I would work one-on-one with people for 180 days.

I focused each month on one of my six foundation fundamentals:

- Nutrition (*not* dieting)
- Movement (*not* exercise)
- Sleep (quality *not* quantity)
- De-stressing
- Hydration
- Breathing

I had realized that most of us had about two of these foundation fundamentals in place, but beyond that, it was a mess. Armed with my novel Awesome180 programme I went out and created the idea of The Habit Coach™. Each month, my clients and I would attack one fundamental area of health, and well-being. I trademarked the term The Habit Coach as I knew way back then that it was going to be huge!

By the end of the first year, I had worked with a variety of clients, industrialists, homemakers, students, first jobbers and CEOs, and decided to launch the podcast *The Habit Coach with Ashdin Doctor*. In a few months, the podcast was on the top ten lists in India and on some very prestigious international lists that had the likes of Oprah Winfrey, Tony Robbins, Tim Ferris and Sadhguru on them. I cried seeing my name next to the likes of Oprah and Tony. Both heroes of mine.

Over 900+ episodes of the podcast have now been aired. This is how my journey towards habit-coaching began. I share my experiences and lessons here—a culmination of all the learning from working with my clients one-on-one; from conducting workshops with over 2,500 participants and learning from their challenges.

This book is more than just about 'understanding habits', it is a guide to creating and then using habits to bring about a real change in your life, just as I did. You are the hero of this book. You are the protagonist. And I, Ashdin Doctor, am your Habit Coach. As your coach I want to show you how you can learn to create the life you want. What are the practical steps you need to take, how change works in the real world, and how can you use these simple learnings to make a change, that lasts for the rest of your life. However, most change seems to come on the other side of discomfort and no one likes to be uncomfortable. So how does one deal with it?

This book shares how change works in the real world. It brings you learnings drawn from my work with my clients; it offers a practical approach for making effortless changes in your life. Changes that stick because you learn—through choice and with awareness—to make them into habits.

Most importantly, this book breaks down the critical 'Hows' of habit change:

- How to form new habits.
- How to make a habit a part of our everyday life.
- How to break habits that no longer serve you.
- And how to do all of the above in a way that is uniquely designed with and for you, to make the experience zestful and doable.

There have been some brilliant books on habits that have paved the way for what I do now. *The Power of Habit*[1] by Charles Duhigg introduced concepts like the 21-day rule to form habits and the habit loop. *Atomic Habits*[2] by James Clear was published just a month after I started Habit Coaching. It discussed many important concepts like making small changes to form a habit that I was already using in my coaching programme. Reading this book, I felt validated—I was on the right path. But I felt one important question was missing; what happens when you still feel frustrated after trying all these concepts? After all some of these are difficult to implement in your everyday lives.

Here's where my experience as a Habit Coach comes in handy. Having worked as a Habit Coach for over six years, I know the pitfalls—places where existing theories of habits break down, where frustration sets in—and where success lies.

As your Habit Coach, I will keep sharing stories with you from my life and the lives of people who have benefited from these techniques. It is important for you to see how we have used them in a practical way, so that you can incorporate them into your life as well. Many chapters in the book have exercises to coach you through making the necessary habit changes towards your awesome life. Take these exercises seriously, dedicate a little time for them. Start by getting yourself a notebook and a pen.

You will use this notebook only for your habits and the creation of your awesome life. Write your name, draw in it, make it unique, make it your own. This is your path and your story to an awesome life.

Exercise

In your notebook I want you to write:

- *Three things you have always wanted to change about your life, but were too afraid to start.*
- *Three things about your life that you started to change but failed to complete.*
- *Three things in your life that you set out to change and were successful in changing.*

Step 1: *I want you to introspect on what was the difference/s between the first two categories and the last one. What did you do differently?*

Step 2: *Choose three things you want to change about your life or three habits that you want to inculcate and use this book to bring about a change in only these three aspects of your life. These will be your key focus areas for the rest of this book. I am sharing a list of areas in our life we often need more focus on:*

- *Financial*
- *Personal*
- *Intimate relationships*
- *Professional*
- *Health*
- *Sleep*
- *Studying*
- *Training*

Don't fall into the trap of decision paralysis. I know it seems daunting, but do it. Don't delay. There will always be that fear, which we will discuss in the next chapter.

Understanding Habits

1

What Are Habits?

'You first make the bunny ears, then you cross them over, Ashdin are you watching?' my mother's voice rang, as I sat on the chair crying, tears rolling down my face.

I kicked and screamed in frustration. I had been trying to tie my own shoelaces, but was just not getting the hang of it. I no longer wanted baby Velcro shoes. I wanted the big-boy shoes with the big-boy laces!

My mother patiently started again. 'Now take these two ends and one goes over the other and under…'

Do you remember the frustration? Those damn laces were impossible to tie! Our fingers lacked the dexterity and the skill to tie the shoelaces. Now, as an adult, you can tie your shoelaces while talking to someone and hopping on one foot! Let me ask you. Do you even remember how you tie your shoelaces? It's just another habit executed on autopilot.

We don't realize it but everything we do subconsciously throughout the day, is just a series of deep-rooted habits. Have you ever noticed how some days just disappear? You don't know what happened, you can't remember anything significant and yet the day flew by. What happened was, (just like tying your shoelaces) you lived that day on autopilot. That day was lived through the habits accumulated over the course of your life. My favourite example of this is how we wear our socks and shoes. Do you wear sock-sock, then shoe-shoe? Or do you wear sock-shoe and then the next sock-shoe? This is something I bet you have not thought about in the last few years. Just like tying your shoelaces.

Such actions have gotten hardwired into our brain and become our default methods of navigating the world. Doing things on autopilot is a very powerful tool that helps us preserve energy. Imagine if we had to go through learning to tie our shoelaces every single day! Our habits help us navigate through life. However, most of the time we do not form 'conscious habits'. Instead, we form habits without much thought. We do not evaluate if this habit will help us in the long run—will it be good for us, will it be bad for us? To have that awesome life, we have to build the right habits. There is no way around it. There is no shortcut to success. There is no forcing our way around things. Any sustainable change has to involve habits.

> *'Your habits will determine your future.'*
> *JACK CANFIELD*

This chapter examines how to best approach and think about habits. It is not theory-based and we will not deep dive into the way our brains store habits, or discuss the basal ganglia, or the 'Default Mode Network'. As much as I would love to geek out about it, that is not what we will do here. Instead, I want to give you real-life examples that will make you go, Aha!

I want to discuss how habits are a practical part of our lives and how we can use time as an ally to better our lives.

You will learn that almost everything you do right now in your life, is nothing more than a habit or in some way related to a habit. The *Oxford Dictionary* defines a habit as 'a thing that you do often and almost without thinking, especially something that is hard to stop doing.' I think this definition is too broad and misses some very important nuances. The way I like to define a habit is, as *'An action or thought that is repeated at a set frequency. This may or may not become subconscious over a period of time'*.

Let's break this down. We all typically think of habits as daily actions—brushing our teeth, drinking water, tying shoelaces, etc. However, what we often fail to appreciate is that habits are also the thoughts we have. Imagine waking up every day and thinking, 'Oh no! It is morning, life sucks'. That is a habit! If we wake up every day and think that life sucks, that is how we are going to experience life. Our habits form our lives. Take a minute and think about it, what are the thoughts that you have all the time? These thoughts have become your habits; and yes, we can bring about a change in our thinking habits as well. My definition of a habit also refers to a 'set frequency'.

We often think of habits as things we do daily. However, there are some habits—such as drinking coffee or tea—that are repeated multiple times a day, unlike habits that are brought into play only once a day, like writing in your gratitude journal. We also have habits that show up once a week, for example sitting down to watch a weekly show on television or doing the Sunday crossword. These weekly habits are the toughest to make and the easiest to break, because there is not enough repetition in them. The gap is too long and hence it is harder to form these habits.

The lesser the frequency, the harder it is for a habit to form. So if you want to make exercise a habit make sure you exercise at least four times a week. Most start with thrice a week. Surprisingly, sticking to a four-times-a-week schedule is easier than a thrice-a-week schedule! But for now, worry not. Through this book, you will learn the simple ways in which you can create these habits and be consistent.

The last part of my definition of a 'habit' says that 'this may be or may not be subconscious behaviour'. It is often believed that a habit is something that only operates on autopilot. Like wearing one's shoes. However, not all habits need to be ingrained in the subconscious. For example, exercising is a habit but we do not do it subconsciously. Similarly, fixing a healthy salad a day can be a habit, but a conscious habit. So, remove the notion that all habits need to become subconscious. And as we will learn later in the book there are many ways to make conscious habits run on autopilot as well.

Exercise

In your notebook I want you to:

1. *Become aware of and write down two action habits that you currently do every day without thinking about them.*
2. *Identify and write down two habitual thoughts you have every day that you weren't aware of earlier.*
3. *Think of and write down three habits you would like to create in your life based on the realizations you had from the exercise in the Introduction. After your introspection, I am sure you must have identified a few areas of your life that need work. You can spend some time thinking about these three habits. Don't worry, they are not cast in stone, you can change them again later in the book.*

2

Your 'Habit Train' Decides Your Journey and Destination

When I was a kid, we used to go and stay at our tiny home in the village in Bordi. We would drive there and the road often ran alongside railway tracks. Our car would stop at railway crossings and wait for an incoming train to pass. I used to love seeing these trains thundering past. One engine in front towing fifteen to twenty carriages. My dad and I would try and count the number of carriages as they sped by.

Some trains were longer than others. Some just carried people, others just carried goods to be transported. The beauty of these trains lay in the way they ran on set tracks. Each train knew exactly where it was going and would get there unwavering. No carriage in the middle could get lost somewhere. The engine powered the train, but no power was generated by each individual carriage. They were just pulled along. The beautiful thing about habits is that they are like railway carriages on a train. One habit attaches onto the habit before it and subsequently has another habit that attaches itself after it. This goes on to form a train. As the first carriage moves forward, it takes all the other carriages with it. Just like a train! Isn't it beautiful? I call this 'The Habit Train'. However, in our everyday life, we refer to them as routines. Think about your morning routine for a moment. You wake up, snooze the alarm, then once it rings again you get out of bed and switch off the alarm. Pick up your phone and head to the toilet. You sit on the pot, scroll through your phone, wash your hands, brush your teeth and wash your face. Each of these actions is an individual habit. Together they form a routine. One habit leads to the next, which in turn leads to another.

Slipping a Habit into a Routine: These routines are powerful things because they can string along a habit. If you want to add a new habit into your life it is best to slip it into a routine and watch it being pulled along. Finding the right place to slip it in is important. Making sure it does not disrupt the habits that follow. This is the key part of adding a habit to your life.

Very often we can add a habit at the wrong place in a routine and derail the habit train. In fact, we use this technique very strategically when we try and get rid of our bad habits. Especially since most of us first think of our bad habits when we think about habits at all. So, remember when adding a beneficial habit to the habit train, it needs to be so subtly done that the following habits are not affected.

Habit 1 + Habit 2 + Habit 3 + Habit 4 + Habit 5 = Routine/ Habit Train

Ritualizing Routines: When you continue with a particular routine for a long period of time, you start associating emotions with it. These emotions create an even stronger bond between you and the routine. For many if they do not have their morning tea or coffee routine, they feel cranky or that their day is not going to be a good one. 'Don't talk to me till I have had my first mug of coffee.'

In India, drinking chai is the ritual, the first cup of chai is no longer a habit, it's a feeling. Think about that dessert or piece of chocolate after a meal. It is nothing but a routine that has an emotion—desire or pleasure—attached to it. People who run or go to the gym very regularly, are distressed when they miss their daily session. Missing it makes them feel lethargic for the rest of the day. Something as hard as exercise has become something they yearn for, an emotion so alien to someone who does not exercise.

Routines + Emotions = Rituals.

It is so hard to get someone to change their rituals, because they have an emotion invested in it. Taking it away is like a personal attack. It is like a change of identity.

The idea is to turn our good, healthy, beneficial routines into rituals as soon as possible. This way the chances of you missing them is very low. These kinds of rituals are so important for all of us to have.

Whenever I start coaching a new client. One of the things we do is sit and go through each and every habit, routine, and ritual they currently have for the day. This is a long and detailed process; we go through each action they do and sometimes discuss why they do it. Almost always they look at me in shock and say 'it is so scary to see my entire life laid out in front of me like this'.

> *'We are what we do repeatedly.'*
> *ARISTOTLE*

This is the real 'Aha!' moment for most people. This is when they realize that they are nothing but an accumulation of their daily habits. In that instant, they realize that their current life is a function of all these daily actions and thoughts. The same actions and thoughts that they have been having for so many years.

Let me explain this with an example. Rohit was a struggling entrepreneur when we met. He had spent the last four years on his start-up and was heading to a burnout. His mantra for life was 'I am busy and I can't do all the things I want to do because I am so busy.' His health, his relationships and everything had taken a beating. At my insistence, I made Rohit sit down and write all the things he did in a day. We made a list of his habit and routines. We even listed the kind of work he was doing.

After the second day of noting down his daily activity, I got an SOS call from him. 'Ashdin, I spent the last two days doing absolute rubbish. Looking at what I have written down, it looks like I am just wasting time. Immediately, I can think of twenty ways to improve my time.' And he did. It all started with just noting down his daily habits and routines.

At this point, I would encourage you to pull out a sheet of paper and write down all your habits, routines, and thoughts. See where your life is headed. Is this the kind of life you want to live? The truth is that you can have a very different life from the one you currently lead, if you want it.

Understand that your present life is nothing but the habits of your past. I want you to realize that your future life is nothing but the habits of your present. Use this book to start making these changes in your life. To create that amazing future for yourself. As I like to say 'Awesome lives start with awesome habits'.

Habits + Routines + Rituals = Life

Exercise

I want you to look at your typical day and identify the habit trains that are taking place. Write down how you notice one habit flowing into the next habit.

Can you identify different emotions that exist with each of these habits?

Have any of these habits turned into rituals? Without these ritualistic habits, you feel like something is missing in your life.

These are the habits that will be the most difficult for you to change. So do not try tampering with them as we progress through this book. It is important to identify our current habit trains so that we can add the new habits to these trains later in the book.

3
Habits Are Hereditary

Did you know that Mushroom DNA is closer to human DNA, than it is to plant DNA? Or that the animal with the most complex DNA is the tiny water flea 'Daphnia' which has the most genes of any animal, some 31,000. Compare that to our human DNA at just 23,000![1]

We are so used to blaming everything on our genes. It is one of the easiest things to blame. Well, because you inherited your genes from your parents, it is their fault you are the way you are. How often have we heard people saying, 'I have diabetes because it runs in my family' or 'I will get hypertension because my father also had it' or 'Everyone in my family is fat, it is genetics'. You might have said this as well. Blamed your current state on the genes you inherited from your parents and grandparents.

The truth is that genes aren't your future, written in stone, unchanging. A whole new area of study 'Epigenetics' is teaching us that you can turn genes on and off by changing the environment you live in and the choices you make.[2] This is a fascinating field of study. You may be predisposed to diabetes, but it is not a 'done deal'. If you make the changes needed, you can 'switch off' the genes responsible and go through life without diabetes. Similarly, you can turn on dormant (inactive) genes by making poor lifestyle choices.

The key is that epigenetic changes do not actually change DNA, the DNA stays the same, what does change is the way the body reads the DNA, and hence the outcome changes. Isn't it amazing!

You obviously cannot change the colour of your eyes or your hair or the way your ligaments and tendons connect. But you can change the diseases you would have been prone to. You can change the way your health changes. You can change the quality of your sleep, the way you process stress and the composition of your body, fat or muscle. You will notice one important thing. The conditions necessary for change are nothing but your lifestyle and the environment you live in. In other words, your habits.

Your habits are the key to changing the way your genes express themselves. Your habits are the key to changing what you thought of as a certain fate. Your habits are the key to unlocking the power of your genetics.

Unfortunately, when we inherit our genes, we also inherit something else. We inherit the habits of our parents. Along with everything else, we take from our parents some of their habits as well. In the same way that their parents (your grandparents) passed their habits onto them (your parents).

My grandmother was raised in a very prosperous family that suddenly lost all its money. So, her habits were partly very wealthy, baking sweet dishes every day, changing her clothes thrice a day (one never knows who might drop by for tea); and partly from the life of poverty, very hard working (she used to stitch dresses and do embroidery), very frugal living, didn't want much (she always wore the same set of ruby earrings and a watch).

Hence, she raised my mother in the same manner. Mom had to stitch her own clothes and give tuitions to earn money. But along with the work ethic came something else. My grandmother's love for sweets. To make food taste better she would put sugar on everything. Sugar sprinkled on bread. Sugar on rice was a go-to dish! The tea was sweet. Jam on all the toast and bread.

When I came along, I was brought up in a household that loved its sweet! Everything was sweet. I used to put two spoons (that were not teaspoons) of sugar in my mug of tea—a thought that made many of my friends queasy, but that was normal for me! And I wasn't stopped by my family from doing so. My Grandmum would cook oats and add sugar on the top. We would add sugar to our already sugary breakfast cereal!

My three favourite dishes growing up were crepes or pancakes, a banana milkshake with a lot of sugar and my Grandmum's famous bread pudding. The scent of it still lingers in my memory. The crunch of the caramelized sugar... ah! Heaven. So along with my big nose, I also inherited my sugar addiction. The nose was purely a genetic lottery. The sugar addiction was taught behaviour or my 'Familial Habits'.

Now think about your life. Take a long hard look at all your lifestyle choices and challenges. Do you see a similarity in the way you are currently living and the way that you were raised? Do you notice how the choices you make each day are probably choices you learnt from your parents?

Sleeping late and waking up late. Shouting, screaming, getting angry or being emotionally abusive. Being a couch potato in the evenings. Having a drink every day or smoking. Snacking more than you should. Taking on too much financial debt. These habits can creep into all aspects of your life.

This realization itself is very powerful. You can now finally understand why you do some of the things you do. But more importantly, you can choose to make a change. I like to call these kinds of habits 'Familial Habits'. These are the ones we inherited from our family.

From this day onwards, choose to make changes in your life. Learn to break away from the bonds of these Familial Habits. Using the techniques discussed in this book, learn that you can change the course of your life. It is not always written in your DNA. Using the power of Epigenetics, you can change the way illnesses and disease appear in your body. You are no longer helpless to them. You are in charge, you have the choice, so create the right habits.

I had to change my sugar binging habit. It was a struggle. Sugar was such an emotional crutch for me. I had sugar when I was happy and wanted to celebrate. I had sugar when I was sad and feeling low. I had sugar because it was 'a must' after each meal.

Breaking the sugar habit for me was easily one of the hardest things that I have done. It was one of the habits that brought about the most profound changes to my mind and body as well. My skin tone changed, my energy levels increased, I became more focused and less irritable. Giving up these bad Familial Habits will definitely improve your life. But imagine the effect on your kids and your future generations.

By stopping these habits with you, their lives will be changed forever. You have the power to end this inheritance.

Change your habits from today, and you will be teaching your children new, better habits in their place. Habits that will lead them on a different path of health and well-being. So, who knows, the chronic illnesses that plagued your family up till now might disappear in the next generation. Unfortunately, however, the big nose might still hang on!

Exercise

The habits that we inherit are often responsible for where we find ourselves in our lives. Look at the areas of your life that you have identified as 'needs improvement'. Do you notice habits that you currently have that were probably passed down to you from your parents?

Note the habits that you identified in exercise in Chapter 1. Which of those did you inherit?

Make a list of these inherited habits that you would like to change or get rid of.

4

Fear of Change Vs. Desire for Change

Little Aryan's eyes peeking just above the kitchen counter had a glint in them. His little hands gripped the granite top. He had spent the last half-hour watching his mother, Asha, layer in her special trifle pudding. With each layer he had licked his lips. He wanted to dive into that pudding face first, use of hands optional. The only thing stopping him was the stern voice of his mother, 'Aryan, if you touch the trifle, only God knows what I will do to you.'

I sat on the side watching all this take place. Seeing my friend's six-year-old squirm and wriggle faced with this dilemma was pure entertainment. It was almost as if two people were wrestling within him. One driven with desire for that pudding, the other driven by fear of his mother's wrath.

We are exactly like my friend's son. We are no longer six-years-old, but we have the same wrestling match taking place within us all the time. We have the desire to do something and change our lives. The desire for a better life is burning deep in us. Yet there is a fear of change. The fear of the unknown.

> *'Each of us must confront our own fears, must come face to face with them. How we handle our fears will determine where we go with the rest of our lives. To experience adventure or to be limited by the fear of it.'*
>
> *JUDY BLUME*

Notice that Aryan's mother had not told him what she would do to him, if he touched the pudding. All she said was, 'If you touch the trifle, only God knows what I will do to you.' But it was Aryan's imagination that built up the fears and made them real in his mind.

The very fact that you are reading this book shows me that you desire to bring some change into your life. However small or huge it may be. You might be perfectly happy and content with the way your life is going and that is amazing! But you realize that change is inevitable and change is always taking place. Or you might be in a place of great distress. You want to change everything about your life. You do not like the person you have become and the life you are currently living. And that is okay too.

You can create whatever future you want for yourself. As long as you understand your special relationship with change itself. Each of us has our unique relationship with change. This relationship consists of two opposing forces:

- Fear of Change
- Desire for Change

Let's examine each.

Fear of Change

For many of us, this fear is debilitating. It prevents us from moving forward with our lives. It prevents growth from taking place. We know and see so many people who do the same thing day after day, after day. Some people are genuinely content with their lives. They are happy and living to their fullest doing the same thing. We are not talking about them. We are talking about the people who keep complaining about their lives but do not do anything about it. They want to change their life but are too scared to do it. You hear them constantly complaining. Yet they stay stuck. It is their fear of change that is holding them back and it has become debilitating.

The problem is that the fear of change is an accumulation of many smaller fears (listed below) that join together and keep you stuck with something you are unhappy with.

Fear of the unknown: This is a very primal fear. It is like the fear of the dark. We do not know what is lurking in the shadows. Some people embrace it and become explorers. Others never move out of their comfort zone.

For me, fear of the unknown started disappearing when I started going on high-altitude treks. After walking for about five days, ever farther from civilization, you feel like you are in the middle of nowhere. At least nowadays these routes are fairly well-trodden. Imagine the first people to explore this dangerous terrain.

What we must learn is that the fear of the unknown is only conquered by being prepared. It is like the Boy Scout's motto of being prepared. We basically have to reduce the uncertainty in our life. If we can do that the unknown has no grip on us.

We do this by arming ourselves with the right research, the right tools, and the right skills. Many of these we will cover in this book. But the rule here is, the more you know, the less remains unknown. So be prepared, learn, and explore!

Fear of criticism: This fear can be traced to two places. The first, our parents and family—especially if we grew up in an overcritical house, where everything we did was evaluated and judged and words like good and bad used all the time. Living in a house like that stunts the ability to change due to fear of being criticized, as nothing we do seems to be good enough. The second place that fear of criticism arises is when we are adversely judged socially by our peers and by society. With so much shared and exposed on social media, it is easy to feel vulnerable. The fear of being judged, mocked and made fun of can give rise to the feeling that nothing we do will be good enough. It is important for us to recognize our need for external approval. It is like we are seeking their approval! The way to deal with the fear of criticism is to not seek approval, but seek feedback. If we seek feedback, we approach it from a positive perspective. A positive point of view; it is not criticism; it is fuel to grow!

Fear of the new: Years ago, I was talking to a friend of mine who was in a long-term relationship that had turned toxic. She and her partner fought all the time, threatening each other. When I asked her why she did not end it and move on to someone new, she said, 'Who knows what kind of guy I'll get? I'll have to start from the beginning. It's too much work!'

This is just one example that illustrates how we think of new beginnings. Many of us think about it as work. Starting from zero all over again.

When it comes to new beginnings, two fears hold us back: the first is closely linked to the fear of the unknown, new beginnings are unknown things. However, the more we learn about them and research them the better we feel. The second is linked to the feeling that we are starting from zero and will have to create everything again.

The truth is that *you never start from zero again*. You always start with the experience you have gained from the past. This experience propels you forward much faster! I keep using this example when talking about entrepreneurs. Before I started the habit coaching business, I had started two other ventures. I realized that, every time I started a new business, the learnings from the last business were so relevant and I could create and make decisions much faster. Each new thing I start now takes less time and effort to do. This is because of all the experience I have gained! Similarly, in most things, you start again or anew. Realize that it will be easier the second time around, if you learned from the first.

Can you convert your fear of the new into excitement? If you can be excited about the new change, the fear will no longer have a grip on you. The excitement will push you forward towards that change you are seeking and looking for.

Fear of pain and discomfort: There is no better example of this fear than getting an exercise routine in place or the habit of a cold shower. Both are very uncomfortable. In fact, most change at some level is uncomfortable or causes pain. Getting out of a relationship is a change, the conversations leading up to it are uncomfortable and pain definitely follows. Similarly, if you want to start a side project and become an entrepreneur, you will have to work longer hours. It is uncomfortable to do. It is painful to say no to your family when you have to work late. However, these are things we do because they need to be done.

The fear of pain and discomfort can be minimized dramatically in two ways. The first is by getting comfortable doing uncomfortable things. Putting yourself in uncomfortable situations routinely can make you more resilient and helps deal with the change. The second is by making a very small change at a time, not a dramatic or drastic step. This way you are able to slowly change. It's like turning the heat up gradually by mixing cold and hot water, instead of turning on hot water at max and getting scalded. The more gradual the process, the less likely you are to feel that pain or discomfort. You are stepping out and gradually expanding your comfort zone.

Do things that gradually expand and grow them. Habits are the perfect way of expanding or stretching your comfort zone as you can make small changes that are sustainable for long periods of time. This way the comfort zone slowly grows bigger. We will talk more about this when we discuss the Golden Rules of Habit Change.

Fear of failure: It's called 'atychiphobia'. And if you want to practice failing at something, try pronouncing it! The fear of failure grips us all. It paralyses us because we are so conscious about failure. All through our lives we are taught that all actions end in either success or failure. Win and get celebrated or lose and sulk or worse yet, get made fun of. The most common way out is by not participating. How many times have you refused to participate in something because you thought you would be so bad, that people would make fun of you? The fear of failure prevents you from starting. And starting is the most important part of creating change.

> *'The secret to getting ahead is getting started.'*
> MARK TWAIN

So, the way to overcome this fear of failure, is to give yourself permission to fail. 'I will give it my best and aim to win. But if I can't, then it is ok as well.' You will notice that when young kids play, there is no concept of winning or losing. They play for the fun of it. In the same way, when we try to make that change in our life, we have to play for the fun of it. If kids fall down while playing, they just get up and start again. They try, try, try till they succeed. I use this approach. This is the first book that I am writing and it took longer than I expected. There were many rounds of reviews and feedback that helped me improve the book. And I learnt so much from the process of writing it! Similarly, failure is nothing but a learning step for us. We must give ourselves permission to fail because, in reality, that is like giving ourselves permission to learn!

Permission to fail = Permission to learn.

Fear of success: If fear of failure prevents us from starting, the fear of success prevents us from completing. It's a strange fear to have and seems like such a silly one. Why would someone be scared of success? Well, for many reasons: (i) it might lead to higher expectations the next time; (ii) it might mean being thrown out of one's current social circle (think of someone getting promoted at work and becoming their friend's boss); and, (iii) it might lead to more work and effort in the future. Now think of the number of projects you have taken on and not completed. Think of the times you made what you were doing so hard for yourself that you had no option but to fail, or leave it incomplete. Very often, one way of dealing with this fear of success is to give ourselves impossible goals to achieve. This is called self-sabotage and we do this to ourselves all the time.

A very strict diet and exercise routine is an example of self-sabotage. Many people who say they want to lose weight and get the body of their dreams, are petrified of achieving this dream body. They are scared of the hard work needed to achieve it and to maintain it afterwards. So, the sneaky mind subconsciously chooses a path of failure. It sets a goal that is too hard and a diet that is impossible to stick to. This way when they fail, they can say, 'at least I tried'. As you can see this 'fear of change' is very strong in all of us. I am sure some of these fears were 'Aha! Moments' for you. See which of these fears are holding you back from the life you want and deserve. What is preventing you from taking that first step and making that change. Remember most of the fears are nothing but our imagination going on a wild ride. So, all we have to do is take small steps to rein in the imagination and dismiss the fears.

Desire for Change

There is a never-ending tug of war match between the desire for change and the fear of change, pulling us in opposing directions. We want today to be better than yesterday. We want to see progress and growth in our lives. After all, that is what some of us believe the purpose of life is. To keep growing and having new experiences. If both the desire for change and the fear of change are strong within us, it leads to tremendous frustration. We are unable to decide which of the two to follow. For many of us, our desire for change is not strong enough to push us into action. This is why we do not change. We all know people like that, who do not change for years and eventually get bitter at their state of life. I wish you never reach a point where you are bitter with your life. Where you look back and feel you wasted it.

There are also those who are never satisfied and jump meaninglessly from one desire to the next. Once this person was me. Looking for the next conquest or the next best thing. At the end of the day, a feeling of emptiness was all that remained. This is because the desires so strongly craved, were not meaningful to my life. They did not hold any purpose. It is what I 'believed' I wanted, without giving much thought to it. For you it could be the same, or even what you 'believe' society expects of you, for example, getting married and having a child, or becoming a doctor/a lawyer/an engineer, or running a marathon, or winning competitions.

Pursuing all these things requires a lot of changes in our life. We have to quite literally become this new person. Very often we pursue these things without asking ourselves if we really do want it, or do we just 'believe' it is expected of us. The desire here is external. It is about pleasing others. It is about how we will feel with the praise of others or society. These kinds of external desires are not the strongest when it comes to us creating a change in our life. I often get people writing in saying 'I want to start waking up at 5 a.m. because I have heard it is good. But I don't know what to do when I wake up at 5 a.m.'. This is an example of an external desire for change. We see someone else doing it and we believe we need to do it as well.

Your *own* desire to change, is clearly the most important thing you need on this journey. Making sure it originates from the right source—internally—is critical. The key is to always remember that an external desire to change is fuelled by Motivation, while an internal desire to change is fuelled by Intention.

Exercise

As your Habit Coach, I want you to become familiar with your fears.

Identify which fears are holding you back from achieving the changes in the three aspects of your life you are focusing on.

Different changes you desire might have different fears. They could also be a combination of fears. Once you understand these fears, it is easier to get rid of them so that you can move towards your awesome life.

Getting Started with the Habit-Change Journey

5

Don't Break Your Comfort Zone, Stretch It

One of the most common things you hear with regard to change is, 'break out of your comfort zone'. Motivational gurus shout it out at the top of their voice. It sounds like such a hardcore concept. Like a bird breaking out from its egg and ready to fly, or a butterfly bursting out of its cocoon. These are very energetic images and it is easy to get sucked into the game of breaking out of your comfort zone. Common break-your-comfort-zone activities include bungee jumping, parachuting, etc. Initially accomplishing such feats gives you an adrenaline rush plus an upsurge of confidence, both of which can be addictive (but are temporary). You want more and more of it. You are egged on by the use of terms such as 'grit' and 'determination' by your motivation guru. Go for it! they say, and you do.

Breaking out of your comfort zone in this manner will ensure neither long-term change in your life nor in your habits, but will guarantee exhaustion followed by emptiness as you look for newer and newer activities that give you an adrenaline rush. Your net gain will not be much.

Most of us get swayed by the rush, instead of keeping our eyes on the prize, which is long-term change that can transform our lives.

Must a Comfort Zone Be Broken?

The United States Navy Seals are America's elite special forces. The best of the best. In order to become a Navy Seal, trainees have to pass a five-day test that puts them through the most gruelling time of their life. They get four hours of sleep in all, and are fed very little food while they run, swim, exercise, carry logs and heavy boats and float for hours in the freezing cold sea during those five days. They have no idea what their next task is going to be. They can only imagine the horrors that the trainers have in mind. This five-day selection test is famous as Hell Week.

This is what it would feel like if you had no comfort zone. Where every day was blank and testing you to your limits. The Seals talk about how important that mug of coffee is, or resting on someone's shoulder for just a few precious minutes. These are just small hints of their comfort zones that they crave during Hell Week. These small comforts help them recharge just a little bit. So, you see the comfort zone plays a very important role in our life. It is where we recharge and rest. It is where we feel safe and secure. It is where anxiety goes to sleep.

Our comfort zone houses all those activities, thoughts, people, and environments that make us feel safe, lower our anxiety or appear familiar enough to make us feel comfortable. A large part of our comfort zone is nothing but the habits that keep us comfortable, safe, and secure. Their familiarity means that we do not have to keep thinking about them. Most of them may be done on autopilot.

In other words, our comfort zone is a large part of our life. It is what keeps our life ticking along smoothly. If we did not have a comfort zone, we would feel like we were trapped in a war zone. Our stress and anxiety levels would go through the roof. In other words, our days would be unstable and filled with insecurity.

As opposed to Hell Week for aspiring Seals, the problem that most of us face is living out our entire lives within our comfort zones. If 90 per cent of our life is spent this way, we are not growing, not having any new experiences. New experiences allow us to learn new things, make mistakes and grow! Mistakes are a part of growth.

As your Habit Coach, I want you to keep trying new things. See what works for you. Then identify how these new experiences can turn into future habits. Your current habits define the life you are currently living. Your future habits will define the life you want to live. How will you know which future habits work for you or not? The only way is to try them out.

Stretching the comfort zone: I like to visualize this as an expert chef tossing a pizza. The dough starts off as a little ball. He presses it and expands it. Then he stretches it on the table as far as it will go without breaking. Next he carefully and lovingly kneads it. Then when the dough is ready, he tosses it up in the air. With each toss, it keeps growing bigger and bigger. But it does not break!

That is exactly what stretching our comfort zone should look and feel like. The first time you stretch it, go slow. The dough is not ready yet. Then expand it slowly and carefully. Once you are comfortable with stretching your comfort zone, increase the speed. Toss it up in the air and let it fly. You will notice expanding your comfort zone becomes almost a daily practice.

Expanding and growing existing habits: The trick to stretching a comfort zone is to expand and grow existing habits—the actions and thoughts you have each day, the schedule and routine that you currently follow. The idea is to pull on an existing habit just a little bit. Just enough for the outcome to be slightly new, but keeping the habit still very familiar. The keyword here is familiar. If it does not feel familiar, or if you need to struggle, you have stretched it to the point of breaking. This is the key to growth and sustainable habit change.

A daily dose of grit and determination: Many of us want to start waking up earlier. This is a goal that has become a medal of honour for the 'ultra-productive'. I remember reading about how waking up at 4 a.m. was the key to success. This was many years ago before I understood the concept of habits and gradual change. I immediately set my alarm for 4 a.m. When the alarm went off, I felt I had slept for about five minutes. My eyelids felt like lead. I went to the gym by 5 a.m. The lights were off and the gym trainer lay asleep on one of the benches. That day I nodded off at every meeting I had planned. The day was a washout. Clearly, this was not the way to do it.

I had stretched and broken my comfort zone.

I still get messages from people asking me, 'How do I start waking up at 5.30 a.m.?' What most people do is set their alarm for 5.30 a.m. and change nothing else in their life. This sudden change from 8 to 5.30 a.m. only breaks their comfort zone and not much else. They can use grit and determination for a few days or more to get up at this time, but their motivation will eventually peter out.

I tell them to stretch their comfort zone by waking up just thirty minutes earlier each week. This adds thirty minutes to their morning routine giving it a more relaxed feel. They don't have to think about how to fill the hours from 5.30 to 8 a.m. (the time their day normally got underway).

By setting a goal of waking up just thirty minutes earlier, they are able to make it a habit in a little over a month without too much stress and in a peaceful manner. They do not have to undergo the anxiety and stress of forcing a daily break-out of their comfort zone by summoning up grit and determination. By stretching the comfort zone just a little, a beneficial long-term change is triggered without collateral damage.

The role of challenges: Once in a while, however, breaking out of your comfort zone is necessary. We can try this in the form of a challenge where we do a particular activity for a set period of time. For example, a thirty-day no sugar challenge is something I urge people to do very often. We have had thousands of people do it in the past few years. Another way to challenge oneself is to do something hard once or twice a month, it could be something that you find extremely scary and difficult to do, but feel the need to overcome. For example, I have a fear of heights. Hence, I look for opportunities that will help me challenge this.

A few years ago, I went to learn how to do the flying trapeze in London where one hangs upside down from a bar, while flying through the air, a few floors above the ground. It is a very scary thing to do especially when you have a fear of heights. This way I broke out of my comfort zone, used grit and challenged myself. However, I cannot challenge myself every day like this. That would be a very tiring and exhausting life indeed.

Another way I like to challenge myself is by going on high-altitude treks and summiting various mountains. It is scary and pushes you to your limits, these lie way outside of your comfort zone. So, breaking your comfort zone is good, but when done in the right way and once in a while. For the rest of the time practice stretching your comfort zone by working on your existing habits.

The best way to practice stretching your comfort zone is by using The Three Golden Rules of Habit Change that are explained later in the book.

6

Motivation and Change: Not As Linked As You Would Think

This chapter tells you what motivation cannot do (create that long-term positive change we are after), why it cannot bestow long-term change, and the pitfalls we face if we try to higher the levels of motivation to change. In fact, I'd go so far as to say that the biggest mistake is to rely on motivation and not habits, to make a change.

Most of us typically derive motivation from the outside world (technically dubbed: extrinsic motivation) and it comes in two main forms.

#1. We see someone's success and want that for our own: We see a beautiful, fit body on social media and immediately want to achieve it. We see someone in a sexy red sports car, the top-down, the wind in their hair and we wish it was us.

The root word for motivation, is motive or the cause behind an action. When we derive motivation from the outside world it begins by giving us a feeling of lack in our lives (I want to be like that but am not, and want those things but do not have them). Next, it makes us feel bad about ourselves to the point that many of us feel we are not worthy. It takes root as a negative feeling that brews in us and it is wanting to get rid of this negative feeling that pushes us towards our glittery goal.

In other words, the need to feel better pushes us.

The problem is that 'the need to feel better' can very soon be diverted into other directions. For example, it can turn into binge eating, or stealing, or maxing out your credit card and taking loans we cannot pay back. All of this just to make ourselves feel better. We may have experienced some or all of these in the past.

#2. Related to praise, and social reward: Also comes from the outside, but is not related to things or experiences. Praise in the form of compliments we got from our parents and teachers as a kid. Or our boss telling us in front of the whole office how well we did last month. Or compliments on the food we cooked. Or the number of followers we have on social media; the number of likes and comments we received for our photographs on social media.

Notice how the likes and thumbs up motivate us as well? Fame and popularity are forms of social reward.

Those of us driven by the motivation for social reward number among our dearest goals: 'being recognized by people on the road'; 'People should know my name'; that 'lifestyle of the rich and famous'.

Both #1 and #2 work brilliantly for some people but for most, this kind of motivation does not last long. It is transient. It comes and goes. You see something and get motivated. A few days later you have forgotten about that thing and the motivation has disappeared. This is why we join a gym on the first of January and stop going on the third of January. This is why we start a diet immediately after seeing a friend who has lost a lot of weight, only to drop the diet a few days later.

Haven't we all been in that situation? Where we started with full gusto, we put our heart and soul into it and then, kaput. Back to our old ways. For a majority of people, this is the motivation we use and hence we fail.

Motivation is amazing at getting us started. But lousy at keeping us going.

Motivation is Like Striking a Matchstick

We strike a match to start a fire, at its point of ignition the temperature of the match instantly jumps up to 700 degrees Celsius. But the match lasts only for a few seconds before it burns itself up, and burns our fingers. Motivation is like that matchstick. It is great to get started, but you immediately need to use it to light something more long-lasting, like a candle or a stove, or a campfire.

Can you imagine cooking a full meal only using matches? It's close to impossible. That is what our lives are like when we only rely on motivation to get the job done. We keep lighting match after match after match. Hoping it will cook our food or get us to our goal. This is why we have to keep looking for more and more things to motivate us.

One of my favourite motivational and sales speakers of all time Zig Ziglar said this: 'People often say that motivation doesn't last. Well, neither does bathing—that's why we recommend it daily.' This is why we have dream boards and vision boards and things like that, because we have to keep lighting the match of motivation every single day. This is why there are so many amazing motivational speakers. They are needed to light a fire in our bellies every day.

I am sure this has happened to you as well. You see a motivational YouTube video, filled with energy, filled with passion, filled with gusto, and are charged up. You want to jump out of bed and take over the world. You haven't felt this alive in ages. Then by evening, the effects of that video have worn off. Life has come back to normal.

It is a great business model for motivational speakers but a horrible long-term plan for us. We keep going back for that next hit of motivation. It truly is a great feeling. I love watching these videos too. They are amazing for creating a spark or a start to the process. However, the key to success is figuring out what you can do long-term.

The key to success is figuring out what you can do long-term: If you cannot do something consistently for a long time, you are going to have short-term results. Ask any serial dieter about this. They will have a 'crash diet' that makes them lose a few pounds or kilos till they are on it and then they put it all back on again.

Once they are motivated to start again, they 'crash diet' again and lose the weight for a second time and then poof it is back again. It becomes an endless loop. This is the same story in all aspects of our life. We have these highs and lows of motivation. Some days, we are so motivated, anything is possible. On other days we are so low and feel like giving up.

One of the questions I get asked the most is, 'Ashdin, I am not consistent at anything I start. I lose my motivation; how do I keep my motivation?' And this is the problem right there. The answer is in the question. You are not consistent because you are relying on motivation. You are not consistent because you decided to do something when your motivation was at its peak! You decided to make a change when you were full of that motivational energy. But you stopped because you ran out of that energy. The matchstick was consumed and it burnt your fingers.

Instead, we need to use motivation just as an ignition for something more permanent. This is where habits come in. As we will see later in this book, habits are the real movers of our life. Habits are where the magic happens.

This is why I very proudly tell people that I am an Anti-Motivational speaker. I am invited to speak at various events for large audiences. I love these opportunities and feel blessed to have spoken at some very prestigious organizations. Often, the person introducing me will call me a motivational speaker, and the first thing I do is correct him, 'Anti-motivational'.

As you will see Motivation is just the start. But real change comes from habits. This is why I created this category of Habit Coaching. When I started there were no Habit Coaches. In fact, when you Googled 'habit coach', you got zero results. Now I am so proud of the fact that people are joining me and becoming Habit Coaches.

Too many of us are relying on motivation to get the job done. We need to realize that it is the wrong tool for the job. We are frustrated because we are trying to make a hole in the wall using a screwdriver, instead of a drill. As soon as this realization sets in, you will understand why I like to say 'motivation sucks'.

Can Motivation and Inspiration Create Long-lasting Change?

The actions taken from motivation are fuelled by inspiration. Remember this line because later on, I am going to show you how habits are fuelled by something completely different.

Inspiration is beautiful, it shows us what the possibilities are. It opens our minds to what we can achieve. It makes us dream. Inspiration makes us want to reach for the stars. Go for the impossible. And that is where the problems begin.

We are inspired by people who have reached the very top of their given field. These are people who have 'made it'. They are an embodiment of dedication, hard work, grit, determination, self-discipline, etc. We read about how hard Michael Jordan practiced. He was the first person in the gym and the last to leave. We read about the top CEOs and their work ethic, working seventeen hours a day. Or how Elon Musk used to read two books a day while he was growing up. We see Iron Man competitions and are inspired to start training.

You see what happens with inspiration is that we only get inspired by the extremes. We see their hard work and set these extreme goals. Hence, this is how inspiration makes us think, 'If they wake up at 5 a.m., I must wake up at 4 a.m. If they run five times a week, I will run six times a week. I will train harder than anyone else. No one will be more hard-working than me!'

Which is great, hard work is the key to success, for sure. However, there is one vital truth that is missing when we get inspired— all those amazing high achievers, did not go from zero to two books a day, or from zero to training six hours in the gym, or from zero to working seventeen hours in a day. They trained themselves to be able to do these things. Starting small and then building their way up to that quantity of hard work. However, we do not see the slow grind they had to go through. We only see the final product and that is what inspires us to create something similar for ourselves.

When we try and use inspiration for setting our goals and our daily targets, we end up creating a goal that is very hard or impossible to do. It is no wonder we fail. It is like shooting ourselves in the foot. This is what I like to call self-sabotage.

Self-sabotage: My favourite story of self-sabotage takes place when a friend of mine, Jessica, decided to get fit! She decided that enough was enough. Through the winter and Christmas holidays, she had been eating like crazy. She had put on a little extra weight. A friend of hers had signed up for a full marathon. She got inspired by this and decided to start running as well.

So, she decided that from the first of January she would wake up at 5 a.m. every morning and go for a 5 kilometre (3 mile) run. Now, this friend of mine had never run 5 kilometres before. Neither had she ever woken up at 5 a.m.! Suddenly, from the first of January, she was going to do both these things? As you can imagine, neither the 5 a.m. nor the 5 km happened. She switched off her alarm, rolled over and went back to sleep.

This is self-sabotage. We do this to ourselves because we feel that our goals need to be worthy. They need to be larger than life. Since we were inspired from these goals, they need to be difficult or extraordinary.

When we tell our friends these goals, they should say 'wow!' That is what a goal derived from inspiration feels like. It should be worthy enough to inspire the person we say it to. The problem with these kinds of goals is that they are so hard to start, that we keep procrastinating. We push them aside or make excuses or say, 'I'll start from next Monday.'

Haven't we all been in this situation? Instead, when we think about creating practical habits, we talk about things that can be sustained for long period of time. The key is in the way we define our goals and our habits. So, look around for inspiration, see what amazing things humans have been able to do. But don't use inspiration to form your daily goals. Don't fall into the trap of self-sabotage. As this can affect your self-esteem in the long run.

When motivation and inspiration mix: When all our goals and activities are led by motivation and inspiration, things start getting out of control. Our mind becomes obsessed with only one task. 'How do I achieve that impossible goal as fast as possible?'

Inspiration makes us set these crazy, huge goals and tasks for ourselves. But the motivation exists only as a short burst. It will soon dry out. Or fizzle out. Hence, we kill ourselves trying to do the impossible, as fast as possible before the motivation disappears. Unfortunately, this is where we spend most of our life. This is why we find achieving goals very difficult and hence we give up. When we live our lives like this, every day feels like a struggle. Every day we feel like we are constantly fighting against ourselves and what we want to do.

If you feel that every day is a battle and a struggle, chances are your actions are being fuelled by inspiration and motivation. You feel you have to spend too much energy pushing yourself to do the things you decided, instead of them just flowing freely and effortlessly as they should. This is where I want to share two big secrets with you. If you understand these, you will never look at motivation and inspiration the same again.

Truth 1: The first is that both motivation and inspiration are driven by outside forces and outside desires. They are not our deep inner desires. For example, when we see people travel the world and we are motivated to do it. It is an external motivation. We see the white sand and the blue sea. We see them smiling and having fun. We wish it was us out there. Give it a day or two and the desire disappears. However, when you talk to travel bloggers, the very successful ones are driven by something else.

Some are driven by the freedom they feel, others are driven by the adventure. Both strong internal factors, that drive them and we will touch upon this in greater detail in the next chapter.

Truth 2: The second truth is about the daily struggle. The very successful people, the ones who inspire us. Our inspirations in life! They don't struggle every day and feel that every day is a battle. Don't get me wrong, they work and train extremely hard. But it is not a struggle because they don't force themselves to do it. Their level of output has been achieved after years of consistent practice. They all started small and easy, over time they got better and better.

The daily actions of the people we admire are not forced; they are habits. It is a part of their daily routine. From the outside, we only see the finished product and think it is impossible. However, it is consistent work that has gotten them there, consistency in the form of habits. Nothing will ever replace the hard work needed to be successful and change. But what helps is if we don't have to deal with the internal struggle and can get on the task immediately.

In the end: The objective of this chapter is to show you that you have the ability to create that change in your life. The one you have been dreaming about. You have the ability to succeed in your goals. However, the tools you have been using so far are not the right tools for the job.

So far you have been relying on motivation to keep you going, however, it is like a match that stays lit for a rather short time. And relying on inspiration, forces us to create goals and tasks that are larger than life. Worthy goals because they have been born from inspiration, but these kinds of goals lead to self-sabotage.

Self-sabotage makes us feel useless because we were unable to do what we have planned. It is a vicious cycle we land ourselves into. From today, I want this cycle to stop. From today we shall change the way we do things. No longer shall we wait for inspiration or motivation. From today let's focus on our habits!

Exercise

This will probably be the most difficult and most important exercise for you. It is absolutely essential that you do this today without fail.

I want you to write the following line ten times in your journal. I want that repetition to seep into your brain.

'Motivation sucks. I will never use motivation again.'

Write this down ten times before you go to the next chapter 😆

7

The Power of Intention in Habit Change

Some people seem to adopt new habits and lifestyle changes very easily, while others struggle and fail. Ever wondered why? The answer lies in their intention—the 'why' and 'for what' they wanted to adopt that new habit or make that lifestyle change.

An intention can be powerful enough to motivate and inspire. And without a powerful, pure intention, neither motivation nor inspiration can sustain a habit/change in the long run. This is because habits are fuelled by intention. The stronger and clearer the intention, the faster you achieve the change you were after. Your intention is the engine that starts your habit. When you return from a holiday and are tempted to just let loose, finding it hard to get your routine back, it is the power and strength of your original intention that will kick-start it again.

The intention is what helps you get started and a powerful intention is one that is very personal. It is very close to your heart, or one with which you have a strong emotional connect.

Let's look at weight loss, one of the most common areas that people want to tackle. What drives this intention? Most often it is triggered by someone saying something like 'you are looking fat', or because we have a wedding coming up and need to get ready for it, or because one day we looked at ourselves in the mirror and didn't recognize the person we saw there. None of these can be classified as a powerful enough intention, because none of these get to the heart of 'why' you want to lose fat.

To find the real reason to make that change we need to dig deep—**peel away all the layers** until we arrive at the real intention. But going deep is a scary process and often we just scratch the surface and rely on shallow intentions. As we embark upon this journey of peeling the layers away, I want you to keep your mind and heart open. If you can do this well, you are almost there.

The Three-Whys Technique

In order to get to your true intention, you have to keep probing yourself and keep asking 'why' at least three times. But be careful, the word 'why' can also cause a lot of grief and turn into an accusation if used in an incorrect way.

For instance, when you ask yourself, 'Why can't I wake up on time and exercise?' You are likely to think 'It is because I am lazy and good for nothing'. Questions such as 'Why don't I have any friends?' or 'Why am I not earning as much as my peers?' end up being answered with 'because I am not good enough'. The word 'why' is a very powerful tool, and when used incorrectly can cause one to feel low and halt any effort to change.

The incorrect use of 'why' occurs when we use it on ourselves or others in a manner that it turns into an accusation. For example, 'Why did you not take the garbage out?' This leads down a negative rabbit hole, where all things end with I am or you are 'not good enough'. It forces you or the person receiving the 'why' to justify an action, which puts you or them on the defensive. This kind of 'why' is not useful in an interaction with someone else, or with yourself either!

The correct and more productive way to use 'why' is to phrase it minus the negatives (why + can't/don't/won't). So 'do' instead of 'don't':

- 'Why *do* I want to wake up at 5 a.m.?'
- 'Why *do* I want to lose belly fat?'
- 'Why *do* I need to spend more time with my daughter?'
- 'Why *do* I want to stop smoking?'
- 'Why *do* I need to drink 3 litres of water?'
- 'Why *do* I need a gratitude practice?'

Notice the difference in this kind of questioning. The 'why' here is a thought experiment about how your life can change in the future if this takes place. The questions are all about the future and not the past events. What you are doing is using the why to create a vision of a possible future in your mind. This is powerful!

Having rephrased the question, the power of 'why' gets amplified when we do the next step of this exercise.

We ask 'why' again a second time. The second 'why' is asked using the answer provided for the first 'why'. The answer for the first 'why' becomes the question the second time. Hence:

1. Why do I need to lose fat?

Because I feel more energetic and lighter when I lose fat.

2. Why do I need to feel more energetic and lighter?

Because I want to be able to keep up and play with my child, carefree...!

Did you see what just happened? You peeled away a layer of yourself. The losing fat started off as a surface-level idea. But now you can come to something far deeper.

Now, we ask ourselves 'why' a third time using the answer from the second 'why'.

3. Why do I need to be able to keep up and play with my child, carefree?

Because I want to be a good parent and not miss these precious moments.

The answer emerges from deep within, spontaneously. Notice what happened. You have now taken this level of thinking so deep it has touched a very important part of your life. Probably an insecurity that existed. Something about your personality or something you were fearful of.

The deeper you can go, the stronger your intention will be. The stronger your intention, the more likely you are to start and continue your habit. After all consistency is the key.

Let me share a very personal story with regards to intention setting. As you may now know, I used to be overweight and very unhealthy. To the extent that I would lose my breath climbing up just three flights of stairs. I was unable to hang from a bar or do even a single push-up. Every day I would have backaches and headaches. I would sit down at any given opportunity, I thought standing was evil, cause well, it was hard to do.

So, when I started my fitness journey, I started with a very vain goal of wanting to have visible abs. I thought that would be a good goal. This was back when I used to rely purely on motivation like most of us do. I struggled and fought every day to exercise and eat healthily. I started to lose fat. Every morning I had to watch videos to pump myself up and re-inspire me to get my butt to the gym.

Then, there came a point where nothing I did, seemed to make me want to continue. All the hard work I had put in seemed to be slipping away again. This is when I learned about asking why. So I used the Three-Whys Technique.

Why do I want to lose fat?

So that I can be fitter and healthier.

Why do I need to be fitter and healthier?

So that I do not live in pain and get some chronic disease.

Why do I need to live pain-free and without disease?

Because I never want to be scared about my body again.

Do you see how powerful the last answer is? 'I never want to fear my body again.' I should be able to do whatever I want, without worrying about my body and questioning if it is capable of doing it or not.

When you have an intention that is so strong, it is very hard not to do the habit. It is very hard to think of reasons for not starting the habit because the intention is so strong.

Three-Whys is a very powerful technique. The faster you can peel away the layers the better. The more honest you are with yourself the better. Allow yourself to be vulnerable, you do not need to share your intention with anyone. It is purely yours. So, take any change you have wanted to make in your life. Then take a paper and pen. Sit down peacefully and ask yourself the three whys.

Sometimes, it may take more than three whys to drill down to a deep-seated need. That is fine, you can ask 'why' a few more times.

However, sometimes, you might not find a deep strong enough why. If this happens do not force yourself to find one. It is okay. It just means that the change you want to create does not have a strong enough need or want at this point. Drop it. You do not need to spend too much time and energy on it.

For example, this happened with a client of mine when he wanted to start running.

1. Why do I want to start running?

Because all my friends are running. (Notice it was not for health or fitness reason)

2. Why do I need to run because my friends are running?

Fear of missing out. It gives us something to talk about.

3. Why do I need something to talk about?

No clear answer for this.

As you can see the need was not a deep-rooted one. The intention was not strong enough.

Our lives will be filled with the desire for these kinds of changes that are influenced by others but that fulfil no real need in our lives. Ignore these, there are enough other positive changes that will play a bigger role and create a bigger more lasting impact in your life.

Exercise

Setting your intention is the cornerstone of the habit creation process. This is easily one of the most important exercises in this book. Please take it seriously and do it.

For each of the areas in your life that you want to see a change in, I want you to identify your intention. What is at the core? The real reason for this change to take place.

In your exercise book write down the whys.

*Why 1:*________________________________

*Answer 1:*______________________________

*Why 2:*________________________________

*Answer 2:*______________________________

*Why 3:*________________________________

*Answer 3:*______________________________

Do this for all three things that you want to change. If you do not find a strong enough why, i.e., a strong enough intention, drop that area all together and choose something else to focus on.

Remember, when you are passing through a low phase in life, it is this intention that will keep you on the path of your habit. It will make you want to come back and re-start or continue that habit.

Once this exercise is complete, highlight your intentions for the three things you want to change and keep referring to them when you feel low.

The Three Golden Rules of Habit Change

8

A Brief Overview

'Just tell me what to do!' a friend yelped at me, 'I have tried and tried everything.' The frustration was palpable in his voice. 'I just have no idea what to do.'

'How do I remain consistent with the things I start?' he said stirring his coffee. 'I feel like such a loser! I see so many people online being consistent and making changes in their life, but I start and stop.'

Before I started Habit Coaching, a lot of my friends would offer to take me to lunch or coffee and ask for advice on health or stress or how to be more productive, etc. I would tell them what to do and bore them with the science behind my suggestions as well. I am a geek after all. Once they were convinced, they would go off to practice.

A month later we would be sitting again at a coffee shop having a discussion, similar to the one above. That's when I realized that knowing what to do is just one small part of the puzzle. Knowing how to do it consistently is where the gold really lies.

'Ashdin, I am just tired of starting and starting and starting again.'

To which I would annoyingly reply, 'Then learn not to stop.'

After working with my clients, I arrived at just three rules you need to follow if you want to implement any habit. These are distilled ideas, after working and trying various strategies for habit change. They are so effective that when people share their 'new habits' with me, as they very often do at social events, I secretly know that they will fail at implementing them. At first glance, these habits seem perfect and impressive. However, I know they are just too complicated or just too outlandish; we try to achieve too much in too short a time.

The mistake we make when planning habits is that we confuse the habit for the end goal. And for most of us, our end goal is huge. It is just too big or too much of a jump. It is very easy to dream about a new habit that you will 'start on Monday', the problem is that it is not practical. To make your dream work in the real world, you have to plan and create habits in a strategic manner.

When the habit becomes the end goal, it suffers an identity crisis. The goal and the habit have to be separate. If the habit is too difficult to implement on a daily basis, it crumbles under its own weight. Picture an elephant (the habit) trying to balance on a dainty folding chair (your motivation). CRASH!

Instead, I want you to picture habits as the steps on a staircase. Each day you add another step towards the goal. Each step is easy by itself. The smaller the step the easier it is. The larger the step the harder it is. You can choose the size of the step! Each day you take that step towards your goal. The goal is reached by climbing the stairs. The goal and the habits are different!

For many, waking up at 4 a.m. is the goal. Instead of taking steps towards that goal, they set their alarm for 4 a.m. directly and try to wake up. Very difficult. We have all set goals for ourselves in the past that are just as difficult (read, unrealistic). We 'hope' we can achieve them.

Instead of hoping things work, let's build practical habits.

9

Golden Rule #1
Make It Stupidly Small

As we discussed in a previous chapter, all change starts with identifying the core intention. For example, 'I want to be able to sit on the floor comfortably and play with my child without pain and feeling tired'. Thereafter we ask ourselves 'why' multiple times, in the manner described in the previous chapter, till we reach a 'why' that has a strong personal and emotional connect. For the query above, the answer was, 'My body is too rigid and weak at the moment'.

Next, we decide on activities that will help fulfil that intention. For example, doing yoga every day will help with flexibility and strength. Now, most people would have left it at 'doing yoga every day' and then struggled to maintain it as a daily activity. It requires too much motivation and self-discipline to execute. But there are three golden rules that cut out all the angst and struggle, helping you turn that intention into a habit.

This chapter brings you the first rule.

'Stupidly Small' Habits

Whenever you say 'not today' to any such endeavour, it is triggered by the thought of completing the whole, entire activity from start to finish. Our thoughts complete the whole walk or run, and how tired we will be at the end of it, and what a struggle it is going to be. And so we sit frozen and stay in our pyjamas.

What if I tell you that your morning walk or run should not be the actual walk or run. Your 'stupidly small' habit just needs to be putting on your running shoes. That is it.

Once your shoes are on, chances are you will feel like heading out the door for your run. If not, that is cool too. After you put on your shoes, you can sit around and watch TV. Or read the newspaper. But you are going to feel pretty silly doing that. You are more likely to at least jog in place or do a few squats. You might stretch a little and then finally say ok, and head out the door.

By breaking the worthwhile habit we want into a series of 'stupidly small' habits—so small and so tiny that each habit feels almost insignificant, so small and tiny that you require no motivation and no self-discipline to practice the habit, and so small and tiny that you feel stupid not doing it—you end up doing it.

A 'stupidly small' habit is very powerful. It removes the need to force yourself to do anything. It removes the need for motivation and determination.

So, if you want to begin practicing yoga don't think in terms of a full thirty-minute yoga class. That is too long. Any day on which your child is crying and you are running late, you will just ditch the idea completely and get no yoga done that day.

So, here's your 'stupidly small' habit: just roll out your yoga mat and sit on it. That is it.

You will notice that just sitting on it will make you feel like stretching a little. You might decide to do a few Surya Namaskars (Sun salutations). You might decide to do a few plank variations or just chill in downward dog. Notice, the habit is not, 'do yoga'. The habit is, just 'sit on a yoga mat'.

The beauty of starting stupidly small is that it allows for any and all different definitions of what 'stupidly small' is. A physical training instructor practicing for twenty years will find doing twenty Surya Namaskars every morning, 'stupidly small'. While for a less physically-fit beginner it could be just rolling out the yoga mat. The idea is that the habit grows along with you. You keep the habit growing, as you grow and become better at it. The key is that whatever action you choose should feel stupidly small at the time.

For example, my stupidly small habit for writing this book started with me just starting the Pomodoro timer on my browser and opening the document that I was working on. That was the first stupidly small habit. There were days when no idea or thoughts arose. That is when I re-read what I had written earlier. Then there were days when I wrote 700 words at a go in little less than half-an-hour.

My next stupidly small habit—added to starting the Pomodoro timer on my browser and opening the document that I was working on—was to just sit and work on the book, no structure on how much or how long.

When this became easy and a daily practice, I gave myself the goal of 500 words a day. Then when this became easy to do, I upped it to 700 words a day. I grew with my habit. All the while feeling that the habit was 'stupidly small'.

Now, for many people writing 700 words a day will seem like a huge task! And it felt like a huge task to me too when I started writing for the first time. However, since I started stupidly small and continued to grow with it those 700 words now feel easy-peasy! It requires no discipline or motivation to get them done.

I often joke with my clients, that when starting stupidly small, baby steps are just too big. If you see a baby taking its first steps, you see them struggle and fall often. It's hard learning how to walk and babies have a lot of grit and determination to begin walking. Clearly, babies are more hardcore than we are as adults. If we struggled as much or fell as often when trying to learn something new or make a change, we would have given up. Hence, baby steps are too big.

I want your habit to be so stupidly small that you never feel the need to use grit or determination ever. If you catch yourself saying, 'not today', then the habit is not small enough.

Shining Examples of Stupidly Small Habits:

- Pouring a glass of water the night before, to drink in the morning.
- Rolling out the yoga mat.
- Sleeping just fifteen minutes earlier than usual.
- Thinking about one thing you are grateful for, before sleeping.

Pro Tip: The goal or final habit that you want to create usually has a 'first step'. This is where most of the failure-to-start occurs. Break that first step down to a set of 'stupidly small' habits. This first step then breaks the inertia to go further. This first step starts the momentum needed to continue.

In some cases, there are a number of roadblocks that prevent you from taking that first step. This is where the next golden rule comes in, which we look at in the next chapter.

Exercise

For each of the intentions you have created in exercise in Chapter 7, what is the first stupidly small habit you can create? What is so small to do, that you will feel stupid not doing it?

Write the first stupidly small habit for each in your notebook.

Habit 1: I will do ______________________________

Habit 2: I will do ______________________________

Habit 3: I will do ______________________________

Remember, this habit will grow and change and evolve with you.

See what is the smallest action you can take towards the habit right now.

10

Golden Rule #2
Make It Extra Easy

While on the surface making a habit 'easy' sounds very similar to making a habit small, they are two very different things. When we make a habit stupidly small, we are looking for the smallest possible action we can take towards that habit. When we look at making something 'extra easy', we are looking at making that habit as effortless as possible. There should be no effort in executing it. If the habit is hard to do, there is an effort needed.

Our goal with this Golden Rule is to remove all the unnecessary friction that stands in our way from executing the habit.

Let's take the example of the yoga mat and the yoga habit. It is a stupidly small task to place the mat on the floor and sit on it. However, if you have to first climb on top of a stool and reach for the mat that you keep on top of your cupboard, just so that you can roll it out and sit down on it, that isn't going to happen. Climbing up on a stool to get the mat is just too much friction. It makes the stupidly small habit very hard to do. It takes effort.

Similarly, most of our healthy food is hidden away in the cupboards, and the vegetables are in the bottom drawer of the refrigerator. It is very hard to eat these foods because there is just so much friction en route to them, while junk food is usually easily accessible and at arm's reach.

Look at the habits you have tried to create in the past. How much friction existed, hence how much effort was needed to get it done? Was it possible to beat the friction?

We can categorize friction in the following ways.

Environmental friction: This is when the world around you makes it hard or difficult to execute the habit. For example, keeping the yoga mat on top of the cupboard. Or trying to eat healthy when you are surrounded by cookies, donuts, and ice-cream!

Most of the friction we encounter towards making a successful habit extra easy, falls into this category.

- Having a TV in the bedroom makes it hard to go to sleep on time or spend quiet time with your partner.
- If your gratitude journal is kept under a pile of junk and you can't find a pen to write in it, that is friction too.
- Having bright lights at home that disrupt your sleep at night is again environmental.
- Choosing a gym that is thirty minutes away from home is friction. It will take too much effort to drive there and back every day, no matter how good the facilities are. Your gym should be no more than five to ten minutes away from your home or office.

All these are physical changes you can make to the world around you, once a change is made, the friction disappears and it is 'extra easy' to build your new habit.

People as friction: Very often the people we are surrounded by can also play the role of friction in our lives. I remember joining the gym with a friend. We decided that we would push each other to go to the gym. However, every time we decided on a time to go he would say 'not today' and then try convincing me to not go as well.

A client of mine had a co-worker who would keep disturbing her during meetings or when working on an important project. This completely broke her habit of trying to create focused work time. If you want to be strict with your food and eat clean, it will be close to impossible, if you are staying with someone who orders in pizzas and eats junk food all the time. In one case, a client's husband would make fun of her every time she tried to make a healthy choice of some kind. This was very demoralizing. This too is a form of friction. People can play all sorts of psychological games.

There are only two ways that you can remove people as friction from your life:

- Slowly remove them from your life, e.g., not going to the gym with that friend of mine who tried to talk me out of going to the gym every time.
- If you cannot remove them from your life, try and get away from them during the time you want to practice the habit, e.g., find a quiet place to work from where the colleague at work cannot disturb you.

Both ways ensure that they won't act as friction to the process. However, there is third (sometimes less easy) way, and that is to make them your accomplice. Ask them to help you and join you on your journey. For example, you can ask your partner to make sure you sleep on time and request them to turn off the lights when it's time for you to sleep.

When I was forming the habit of not eating desserts, I asked my family not to bring home any desserts. This way it reduced my temptation to eat the desserts and I became accountable to the family.

Established habits as friction: The habits that you have already established, can come in the way of you starting a new one. These habits are part of already formed routines and hence difficult to get out of and add friction to your journey. They make the new habit hard to do or add a few extra steps that would have otherwise been unnecessary.

For example, mothers of toddlers find it hard to add an exercise or yoga habit because their routines for the day are already so tightly set. They can't figure out what to swap for this new habit. To resolve this friction they can do their yoga routine in the room where the child sleeps. This way they can still be around their child, and manage to do yoga or exercise. So the yoga habit can overlap with the child's sleep time.

For some couples, the only time they get with their partners is late at night, which is when they sit together and watch TV or talk to each other. Which is great until they decide they want to end their day earlier. But by doing so they will have to sacrifice the time they spend catching up with each other.

My suggestion is to switch the TV viewing for a pre or post-dinner stroll or a brisk walk. They can then call it a day and wake up earlier to spend extra time in the morning together.

You have to re-engineer the old habit before working on the new habit.

For example, most people find it easy to give up breakfast when they start their Intermittent Fasting habit. However, what they find very difficult is giving up their milky tea and coffee. There are so many emotions associated with that habit of a good cup of morning chai or a coffee.

They first have to be okay with having plain black coffee and green tea with no sugar. Only then can they start the intermittent fasting habit.

Lack of knowledge as friction: In some situations, the more you know about a topic, the easier the habit can become. I realized this when I started my exercise journey. Till then I had always relied on the advice of friends or people in the gym to tell me what exercises to do. Hence it was a constant struggle with no results. However, once I started learning the science behind exercise physiology and the various techniques, the results came faster with lesser effort.

I was able to reduce twenty minutes of cardio, which I hated doing and would often skip, into just four minutes of a Tabata Exercise. Then I learnt about the slow exercise pattern from a book called *Body By Science*.[1] All this dramatically reduced my exercise time, making the habit extra easy!

The more you know, the easier a lot of activities can become. The friction and struggle goes away. Want to improve your sleep, learn about circadian rhythms. Want to improve your productivity, learn speed-reading or scheduling. Want to improve your relationships, learn about love languages.

This is why I created the podcast *The Habit Coach with Ashdin Doctor* and The Habit Coach – Awesome180 YouTube channel as well as this book! The idea is the more you know the faster you grow! Each of the three is packed with knowledge that can help you reduce the friction in getting your habits in place. So become curious about the activities you want to add to your life.

Pro Tip: Every time you think of starting a habit, ask yourself 'How can I make it easier?' Every time you do the habit or action, ask yourself how this could have been easier. Where does the friction lie, when does it occur?

You can select a special place for each habit. You can put the things you will need for that specific habit out in the open where you will see them and remember them.

Exercise

Now for each of the habits that you have identified in the above exercise in Chapter 9, I want you to close your eyes and visualize doing the stupidly small action. Then identify all the friction points along the way.

For each of the habits, I want you to write down what could possibly be a point of friction and a solution for it:

Habit: Roll out the yoga mat

Friction: The yoga mat is placed in the other room, in a cupboard/on top of the cupboard

Solution: Keep the yoga mat outside, next to the spot where it is to be rolled out

If you can think of all the possible excuses at this stage, you will have a habit that runs very smoothly later on.

11

Golden Rule #3
Never Miss Two Days in a Row

This final rule is all about creating consistency. The secret to making habits work for you. A habit without consistency is no habit at all.

When I started learning about habits, the thing everyone was talking about was a 'habit streak'—the habit must be done without a single miss for a set number of days, usually twenty-one. This streak was believed to be the only way to make any changes to a habit. All sorts of techniques were used to ensure one stuck to the habit streak—rewards each day; punishments for not doing the habit. They were basically using the carrot-and-stick approach for habit change.

Did it work? Sure, it did, for people who had already created a similar habit before, or for people who had a lot of grit and determination and hence looked at it as a challenge. However, challenges exist only for a finite period, while habits are meant to work for you for the rest of your life.

I have always felt that the habit streak approach is too robotic or mechanical. The biggest problem with it is that it does not allow for the 'human-ness' of life and hence habits. It does not take into account that we are human beings and hence imperfect. We will make mistakes. We will have good days and bad days.

Not all of us long for or are going to have such a regimented life, almost as if we were in the army. In fact, this idea of a regimented life is something that scares most people. I have lost count of the number of people who told me that their biggest worry of working with a Habit Coach is that they will have a regimented and boring life. For many, this is the result of looking at habits as something that are forced upon you every day, and you face a punishment if you don't (even guilt-tripping would count here).

Clearly, a regimented life is not a practical life. Hence, a regimented approach to habit change, is not a practical approach to habits.

I like to think of habits as a way to create structure and better choices. Not regimentation. If we want to be practical, we have to allow for the mishaps and the days we just don't feel like it! We have to allow for life to get in the way—a sick child you need to take care of, or a party you went to the night before.

> *'Success is neither magical nor mysterious. Success is the natural consequence of consistently applying basic fundamentals.'*
>
> E. JAMES ROHN

There will be times you want to create an 'eating clean healthy food habit' but you end up going to a wedding. It's okay, eat and enjoy the wedding food. The next day make sure you get back on track.

The problem with being compassionate and allowing for mistakes is that we can end up discontinuing the habit. A day's break becomes a two-day break which can turn into a whole week off and then you have to start all over again from scratch. Have you ever experienced this? The best example for this is cheat meals. Very often we allow ourselves a cheat meal, which then turns into a cheat day. Before we know it, it has turned into a cheat week! I absolutely know you have experienced this!

What happens here is very interesting.

Making an excuse for not doing a habit, it is okay once. If you repeat the excuse a second time, you just turned the excuse into the new habit. As a result, you get better and better at making excuses! The excuse is the new habit!

This is why we have to be very careful about the excuses we make. We also end up justifying them: 'I can eat a brownie because I exercised today.' Does that mean every time you exercise you will eat a brownie? You realize that eating the brownie is now the new habit!

I have heard ridiculous excuses like, 'I can't exercise today because I don't have my matching T-shirt and shorts.' We become so good at making excuses that the real habit we wanted to create is left in the dust. We all know people like this, who are masters at making excuses. They are the ones who will often call themselves 'lazy'. They aren't lazy, they just have a habit of making excuses.

The best way to make sure that this does not happen to you, is by following Golden Rule #3, 'Never miss two days in a row!'

What does this rule practically look like?

- Monday: You practiced the habit as planned.
- Tuesday: You practiced the habit as planned.
- Wednesday: You had to go for a party/or were not feeling well so did not practice.
- Thursday: Under any circumstance, practice the habit. If not the full habit at least just the start, the smallest possible element of the habit, even sit on the yoga mat (remember stupidly small?).
- Friday: You practice the habit as planned.

If you are about to miss the habit two days in a row, I suggest doing at least a tiny bit of the habit, just so your mind connects with taking some form of action. For instance, if you can't read your book, just pick it up and open to the page you were on, read a sentence and put it away. What this does is that it prevents the excuse from winning. You, at least, took some action towards the habit. It was not perfect by a long shot. But like I said earlier, we are not looking for perfection. We are looking for consistency.

So later when we talk about tracking habits, even an imperfect execution of the habit is counted as the habit being practiced. We want to create momentum. Anything is better than zero, and it adds up eventually.

Habits are like voting: Another good way of looking at habits from a consistency perspective is to think about habits as voting. You want to have a majority count, for the times you practiced the habit. You do not want a majority for the times you skipped it or made an excuse. Voting for one side is like taking away a vote for the other side. Just like in our government elections, it is a choice. Both sides are constantly eyeing your vote and promising you amazing things. The choice is yours, who you vote for the most, wins!

Each time you vote for a brownie over a salad, the brownie habit gets stronger. Which is why you have to consciously choose. A good way of thinking about this is to remember you aren't just making a choice for something. You are making a choice against something as well. A double-glazed, custard filled donut is not just a vote towards sugar. It's a vote against health as well. Do you want to vote against your health? A powerful thought.

This is why a good target for habits, is a minimum of four times a week. You will notice that if you practice a habit thrice a week, it is less than 50 per cent. If you practice it four times a week, it is more than 50 per cent. This is why it is difficult to start a gym habit if you go thrice a week. Most beginners unfortunately make this mistake. Monday, Wednesday and Friday. You will notice that this breaks the rules of never missing two days in a row. Saturday and Sunday are skipped. It is difficult to start again on Monday.

The weekly habit: A habit that you plan to practice once a week is the hardest habit to form. You might intuitively think it is easy because you just have to remember to do it once. However, the momentum is not generated. The number of times it is repeated is so low that you cannot grow that habit well.

This is why I don't like once-a-week habits. In fact these are usually support systems for the habits we practice through the week. For example, on Sundays I plan what I will do for the rest of the week. The time I spend planning each Sunday is not a habit, but a support activity for my weekly habits.

So, try and avoid any once-a-week habits, it's a very easy trap to fall into by calling them habits. However, they are just activities you do once a week.

Pro Tip: Use a habit tracker to make sure you visually see the days you have skipped. Remember never miss two days in a row.

Don't keep (re)starting: 'I have to start exercising again'. 'I am so tired of starting again'. This is something that we hear so often. If you are tired of starting, don't stop! If you don't stop, you don't have to start!

I often say that the most used sentence on the planet is, 'My diet starts next Monday.' Even worse, 'I'll do it tomorrow', which is a lie because if you look at the calendar there is no day called 'tomorrow'.

Consistency is key! Once you follow the three golden rules of habit change you will notice that consistency becomes much easier. Don't keep starting again and again. Instead, just don't stop. Let the momentum carry you through.

The beauty is that once you start seeing the benefits of the habit, the rate of change will dramatically increase. This is the way habits compound over time and grow. Every time you stop, you destroy the momentum. Every time you stop, you have to restart. Hence, don't completely stop, find a smaller manageable size for the habit and continue. Even a little bit maintains the momentum.

Exercise

Now I want you to schedule your habits.

Think about how often you will do them. Plan them out Monday to Sunday.

If you are going to be skipping Saturday and Sunday, remember that is missing two days in a row. So ideally try and avoid a situation where you, by design, miss two days in a row.

Write the following in your notebook.

Habit name: Monday, Tuesday, Thursday, Friday, Sunday

If you will be practicing a habit multiple times a day, make sure you write how many times a day you might want to do that habit as well.

Example: Meditate twice a day.

Creating Successful Systems

12

Creating Systems That Work for Us

A friend of mine, Samir, was planning on climbing Mt. Everest. And as most cocky Everest climbers will tell you, the goal is not to climb Mt. Everest. The goal is to 'Reach back down after climbing to the top'. Summiting Everest is such a tough ordeal. The goal is so distant and seemingly impossible. Winds that could swoop you up like a kite. The cold that literally freezes your bits off. The glaciers that shift beneath your feet. The air so thin it makes you delirious. A climb so long that fatigue is your constant companion.

But Everest is the goal. Well... reaching back from Everest, is the goal. I was speaking to my friends who had climbed Mt. Everest and they told me something very interesting. They said they never focused on the goal. 'We never focus on whether we will or won't summit,' they said, 'because while climbing, there should not be a doubt in your mind.'

The goal once set becomes irrelevant. This is because the role of the goal is to just give direction. Once the direction is set you check it once in a while, only to make sure you are climbing up the right mountain. What most of us do is obsess over the goal. We look at the goal every day. We crib about the lack of progress. We wonder when we will achieve it. The goal guides our mood—we are either elated or depressed because of it.

True success does not come from a blind focus on the goal. True success comes from a focus on your systems. The Mt. Everest summiteers tell me that they just focus on one day at a time and all the tasks that need to be done on that particular day. The tasks include checking the equipment, making sure their food and rations are ready, making sure they are exercising and staying physically fit and making sure their bodies are acclimatizing to the thin air.

Every day they have a routine made up of small habits. They practice these habits in a safe environment so that when they are up there, in finger-freezing cold, they know exactly what to do according to the system.

Now I know that you are not planning on climbing an 8,848-meter-high mountain. But the same rule applies to our daily life goals as well. Getting a promotion, losing 10 kilos, finding a life partner, writing a book, going on a holiday, etc., the list is endless. If you want to achieve your goals, you have to create a system for them.

For example, to bake a cake you follow a system. You keep the ingredients ready, then you mix them in a particular order and in a particular way. You set the oven to pre-heat while you mix the ingredients. Then you bake the cake at a particular temperature. You check it in a particular way. You rest it and allow it to cool on the kitchen counter. Once it cools, only then you cut into pieces.

Now imagine you did not have this recipe for a cake. It would have been a hit or a miss. Imagine reinventing the recipe every time you wanted to bake the cake. There would be confusion, disorder and a poor outcome. That's what it is like without a system.

Many of us feel our lives are like that, in a state of confusion and disorder. We feel like our days rush past and we have done nothing with them. We feel like we are constantly trying to catch up with life, but are always two or three steps behind. This is because the systems we currently have in our life are not working. We find that our productivity is dead, we are stuck in a job that is not exciting, and we have a midline that this growing horizontally. All these are issues with the system. But we blindly keep repeating what we do over and over again and then wonder why there is no positive change in our lives.

We have to learn to let go of a system that is not serving us anymore, and try something new. Make a change to the system and you can make a change to your life!

There are three basic steps to designing a system.

1. What is the desired end result? (In the above example, baking a cake.)
2. How will you do it? (List the steps, ingredients, tools, actions.)
3. What comes before and what comes after? (Decide in what order these steps, tools, and actions should occur.)

Visualizing the Process

The best way of creating a system is by visualizing the whole process. Simply close your eyes and see yourself go through each step. Visualization is critical because you will be able to see if you are packing too much into the system.

Visualization also teaches you how to pick up on things that could have been missed. This way you will be able to predict the difficulties, you will be able to see the flaws in the plan. You will be able to make small tweaks and decisions to make the process better. One of the simplest examples of a system in our daily life, is our morning routine. Let's visualize it:

1. Wake up
2. Reach for phone
3. Take phone into the toilet
4. While peeing check the news, messages, emails (get horrified)
5. Put the phone on the counter (after finding a dry spot)
6. Reach for the toothbrush with the left hand
7. Reach for toothpaste with the right hand
8. Open the tube and squeeze out paste on the brush
9. Put the paste away (sometimes forgetting to put on the cover)
10. Open tap with the right hand
11. Wet toothbrush
12. Watch as the toothpaste falls off the brush into the sink
13. Curse life
14. Apply toothpaste again
15. Start brushing teeth (notice how it is always from the same side)
16. Look at self in mirror (pass judgment about self)
17. Finish brushing and wash the toothbrush
18. Open tap with the right hand
19. Rinse mouth with water (trying not to splash)
20. Look at teeth in the mirror (picture every toothpaste commercial ever)

You notice a simple activity like brushing your teeth is a system with over twenty steps. Each of those steps is a habit, e.g., we always pick up our brush with the same hand. We always put the same amount of toothpaste on the brush, etc.

The beauty is that we don't need to focus on the goal of having clean white healthy teeth. We just focus on the system. Reaching the desired goal is inevitable when the system is correct. The best part of a system is that it acts like an anchor and roots your day in place. We don't have to 'plan' to do it, we don't have to 'try' to do it. It just happens. Here's an example. We had gone to celebrate a friend's birthday. It was a wild night! Lots of dancing, lots of tequila shots. When we all came back home it was 4 a.m. Each person found a spot and passed out all over the house.

In the morning, when everyone woke up, their brains were not functioning properly, their speech was still slurred and their eyes looked half dead. Each conversation consisted of a 'huh', 'whaaat', with an occasional complaint of 'why is everything so bright'! But I noticed something interesting. Everyone had fresh minty breath. They were in no state to move or function as human beings but they had all managed to brush their teeth. The system of 'wake up and brush teeth' was so ingrained in each one, that's what they defaulted to. Without thinking, the process played out. They got up went to the loo, brushed their teeth and stumbled out.

We all have days that come in like a storm and want to sweep us away. A hectic day at work. A family member who is sick and needs to be taken care of. A sudden meeting at our child's school. Or a fight with a friend. Our systems are what keep our lives intact and in place during those moments. Developing systems that act like anchors are so critical.

Imagine if we had a system for mental and emotional peace that consisted of a gratitude exercise and a meditation practice. This system would have made the rest of these stormy days easier.

Imagine if we had a system for our physical health, either a morning walk or exercise followed by breathing exercises. This system would have kept our day less manic.

Our lives are filled with systems already; these are 'the familiar bits' in an ever-changing world. These systems are what we default back to when everything else is failing around us. However, most of these systems were created subconsciously. They were not planned and designed to optimize our day and our life. Or give us a better result. As your Habit Coach, I want you to create systems mindfully. Systems that remove the stress from your life, systems that help you grow, systems that support the life goals you have. The more practical we are about the systems and habits, the better the chance of us sticking to them.

So let's create some amazing systems and habits for you!

Exercise

Now we shall create systems for each of the habits that have been planned out. For some of us this will be the most exciting time of the habit creation process because we will be identifying and solving for all the hiccups or problems that we may face along the way.

Take a blank page and write down in order how you will be doing that habit. Just the same way I gave you the example of brushing your teeth. Put down as many steps as it may take. You can even write down the habits you will be doing before and after. In this way, there will be complete clarity for what counts as this habit.

Write down

1. *When you will be doing it?*
2. *How long it will take?*
3. *Where will it happen?*

If you make a very solid plan and a system to match, this habit will become a part of your life in no time and bring you rich dividends.

13

Creating a Harmonious Life-Symphony

The silence was heavy with anticipation. There had just been thunderous applause and the sound of people getting out of their seats and then back into them. But now the auditorium fell silent. The conductor raised his baton up in the air and everyone held their breath. With one confident swoosh of that little stick, the orchestra jumped to life and began the most beautiful melody ever heard. It turned and twisted, it had highs and lows and danced around in the audiences mind. It was amazing how so many people, playing so many musical instruments managed to sync with each other. They didn't miss a beat or forget to play or hesitate when it was time to start or stop playing.

This was the first time I was listening to one of the most famous conductors of our time, Zubin Mehta, in 2016. What amazed me was that we all paid a lot of money to 'hear' the conductor. He was the star of that performance. The applause was primarily for him.

If you are not familiar with western classical music, it is easy to believe that the musicians are in charge. However, the magic comes down to the conductor. There are many roles he plays. Here, I want to focus on just one of those roles—being in charge of making sure the players know when to start and when to stop, when to play softly and when to power in. He is in charge of which instrument comes in first, second and third. The order of play. Without a conductor, the orchestra would still be able to play music, but it would not be in harmony. There would be misses and mistakes in starting and stopping on time. The musicians would hesitate. The beat would be missed and after a while, everything would crumble into a mess.

Though it is the orchestra that is producing the actual notes, the truth is that the conductor is making the music. He makes sure the music he desires, i.e., his interpretation of the piece, is produced.

Suppose we think of the orchestra as our collection of habits. The habits we want to do every day. The violinist is your 'gratitude habit'. The person on the French horn is your 'yoga habit'. The saxophonist is your 'hydration habit'.

Now by themselves, the habits can exist. But we need something to tell us when to do which habit. To remind us that it is now time to start the habit or time to stop the habit. This is where the conductor comes in. What the conductor does for the orchestra, is what 'cues' do for your habits. They are little reminders that tell you when it is time to start your habit. Or when it is time to move to the next habit.

Creating Cues to 'Switch On' Our Habits

A good cue is absolutely essential for maintaining habits. There are days you might not feel like doing a habit or might forget to do it. It is the cue that should charge you up or remind you to do the habit. The cue should immediately make you do the habit.

There are many different kinds of cues you can use. Each of these cues has a different role and style of working. You need to choose the cue that is the most practical for your life and that can help you achieve your habit. Remember don't make the cue fancy. Just make it practical, so it works every day like magic.

Alarm or time-based cues: These are the easiest to understand and create. All you have to do is set an alarm on your phone. Every time the alarm goes off it will remind you of that particular habit. Switch off the alarm and do the habit. This works well for small habits that need to be completed. Things that take a few minutes to complete. You can even keep the alarm ringing while you finish the habit so that you do not procrastinate doing it.

My father has set alarms to remind him to take his medicines. At 11:30 a.m. every day that alarm will go off. It does not matter if he is in a meeting or on a flight. That alarm will fire off and remind him to take his tablets. At which point in time, it does not matter what he is doing, he will stop it and take his tablets.

The only downside is that this alarm can ring in the most inappropriate of times. So, do be careful when you are in a space that values silence and no phone calls are allowed.

Create a rule that you will not snooze the alarm more than twice. Ideally, never.

Visual cues: Visual cues are objects that remind you to do a particular habit. These are the most effective cues to use. However, they need to be planned properly. Some of these cues might require preparation.

Visual cues can be physical objects like clothes, bottles, shoes, post-it notes, calendar entries, etc. Anything that you can use to visually remind you to do something. I was on a one-week holiday and I used the sunset as a visual cue to put my phone away and practice five minutes of mindfulness meditation.

Your imagination and creativity are the best source of inspiration for identifying these visual cues.

Another example of a visual cue is, keeping your water bottle with you at all times so you can sip it every time you see it. Most of us keep our bottles of water in the kitchen, so we have to get up and go there to drink water. But if the water bottle follows you around wherever you go, the chances of you drinking from it is greater. I learned this habit while doing my high-altitude treks. Up there, to avoid altitude sickness, we need to drink 5 litres of water. If we forget to drink water, it can be dangerous. So, we all walk around the campsite with a bottle in our hands. It acts as a visual cue to drink.

Similarly, you can use a post-it note on your mirror to remind you of your gratitude exercise or of your affirmations.

When I was starting my exercise routine, I would leave my gym clothes on the bathroom counter the night before. This reminded me to change into them as soon as I used the loo that morning. (The challenge of course was remembering to place the gym clothes there the night before, but I had a system for that as well).

Visual cues help you navigate your world of habits. You can have visual cues all over the house. I wanted my family to drink hot spice tea throughout the day. This tea has medicinal properties. So, what we did was put a big flask in the middle of the living room and three mugs. Every time we saw the flask it reminded us to drink that tea.

We often see inspirational quotes in hospitals and offices. We started putting them up in our office as well, especially in the washrooms. These acted as a cue to form a habit. The habit here was an inspiring thought. As I had mentioned earlier, habits can be both actions and thoughts. So, when you read a board that makes you think in a particular way, it is forming a habit.

We would normally not associate these quotes hung on walls as habits. But they are. A simple board outside a room like 'Leave your worries and shoes at the door' is a cue that is trying to reinforce a habit in you.

The dangers of visual cues are that they can also be used with malice—propaganda messaging and negative messaging on social media are creating habits in us as well. Hence, be very conscious of your environment and the visual cues that lie there. Apart from the messaging, you might also work in an office that is filled with chocolates and snacks lying around. These are also visual cues to just pick them up and have a bite.

Hence, cleaning up the visual cues in your life is also an important thing to do. Visual cues for habits that do not serve you.

Very importantly, remember to keep refreshing and making sure the cue is still present. I used to keep my morning journal on my sofa, so every morning I would see it and remember to write in the journal. This was a habit I had been following for quite some time and it was fairly set. One day we were having a party at home and I was told to 'clean up'. In the process, my journal was kept away somewhere. The next morning, the cue had disappeared, and along with it my habit.

So consciously, create these visual cues and you will be able to form some life-changing habits.

Habits as cues: My favourite type of cue is to use an already existing habit as a cue. For example, my second cup of coffee is a habit. I use this as a cue to get some sun. I would typically have this coffee around 10 a.m. I use that time to go out by a window or on the terrace and soak in some sun. This way the cue for my sunbathing habit, is the second coffee habit.

As humans, our minds are always looking for what is next. 'What is the next thing I have to do?' is the sentiment that drives the 'habits as cues' idea. If we can formalize and structure what comes next after a particular habit, this way it is easier for us to follow. We are not left wondering what to do next. In the previous chapter on systems, I shared how you can create a chain of habits. One neatly following the next.

A practical way to approach habits as cues is to plan the 'new habit' in the same area or vicinity as the 'cue habit'. So once the first habit is done, it can easily flow into the second. For example, group all the bathroom habits together, all the kitchen habits together. This way one habit can automatically cue in the next.

Another practical tip is to have both the 'cue habit' and the 'new habit' doing fairly similar things. We do this so that we do not have to reset our mindset or mind frame between habits. For example, doing your oil pulling [swishing a chosen oil in your mouth for about few minutes before spitting it out; this is thought to benefit oral care and hygiene] while you take a shower. The shower is the cue habit and the oil pulling is the new habit. Since you are in the process of cleaning yourself it makes sense to do them together or one after the other.

Cue fatigue: This is a very interesting phenomenon that takes place from time to time. Very often we set out the perfect cues and the perfect habits and we are in the process of doing them. The consistency is there, we are not missing two days in a row. Then suddenly out of nowhere, the habit falls off the radar altogether. We just stop doing the habit for some inexplicable reason. When we realize that we have not been doing the habit, we are unable to put our finger on just when or why we stopped!

The reason this takes place is because of cue fatigue. The cue we had set for ourselves has stopped working. Our mind got so used to the cue, that the cue ended up as a blind spot. We no longer 'see' the cue. Let's take the example we discussed earlier for drinking water. You have one particular bottle that you use every day. You carry that bottle with you. It sits on your desk. It comes with you to the lunch table or dining table. Soon, your mind will start filtering it out. You will no longer 'see' that the water bottle is there. If you can no longer see the water bottle, how will it serve as a 'visual' cue for you to use it?

This cue fatigue exists mainly in visual cues and alarm (time-based cues). Habits as cues are so dynamic that the fatigue does not set in as quickly. Hence to make cues practical you have to know how to deal with 'cue fatigue'. So, when you notice the fatigue, start switching up the cues. Or you can do this as a system pre-emptively. For example, use a different water bottle every two weeks. Or move the post-it cue around from one place to another.

For alarm-based cues, change the tone of the alarm every two weeks. This way the cue will always sound new and interesting and fatigue will not set in as fast. Like we mentioned earlier, habits are not about monotony and being boring. You have to be dynamic and add new things to them. Keep growing with the habits and keep changing the cues around from time to time.

Final cues: So, when planning your habits plan your cues as well. This increases the chances of you remembering to start the habit.

Chose which of the three kinds of cues you are most comfortable with. Do you like the alarm-based cues or do you prefer visual cues? I, for example, do not like the alarm-based cues, but my father definitely does!

Exercise

Identify cues for each of the habits you want to create. Be very clear about the cues and test them out. Create the cues if need be.

14

Creating Your Own Habit Systems

Now that you know the basics of habits and how you can inculcate them into your life, let's do a quick recap of what we have learnt so far. Before, I start explaining more awesome things about habits, it would be good to track your process till here.

As discussed in the previous chapter, having a habit system is necessary to form new habits and be consistent with them. As your Habit Coach, I've crunched all the learnings of the earlier chapters and have formed a six-step system for you to form any new habit.

Six Steps to Creating A System:

1. What do you want to change?
2. Intention
3. Habit Train or cue
4. New habit
5. Continue the Habit Train
6. Review and improve

What do you want to change? The first step is just identifying what part of your life do you want to change. What part of your life needs to be improved on? We have already identified this in the exercise in the Introduction. Very often we are unsure and get confused about what we want to change. So clarity here is the starting point of the system.

Intention: Now you know 'what' you want to change. You then get to the stage of identifying your intention. Use the Three-Whys method to identify your real intention (as explained in Chapter 7). Peel the layers until you have the intention that motivates you. It needs to be something so strong that you will feel pain by not doing it. If you cannot find this deep emotional connect with your goal it means that this goal was not so important to you. Forget it. Go back to step one and choose a different goal.

Only once your intention is set, take it to the next step.

Habit train or cue: A new habit has to be closely linked to an already established habit. This is because an established habit gives you that nudge or reminder to do the new habit. It acts like a cue. Just like the carriages of a train, the old habit will pull the new habit along with it. So, identify your habit trains and add the new habit to it. If you do not have a habit train you will have to create a new cue like an alarm or a reminder.

New habit: Now it is time to plan for the new habit. Identify the activity or the thought you want to create as a habit. Then follow the Three Golden Rules of habit change:

1. Make it Stupidly Small
2. Make it Extremely Easy
3. Never miss two days in a row

The chance of you sticking to your new habit will be directly related to the way you create this habit.

Do not be overly ambitious, remember you can always grow with a small habit and make it harder slowly. But if you start with a hard-to-do habit and stop doing it, it will never form or take root.

You can write this habit down in detail and you can track this habit to help make it robust! We will cover how to track habits later in this book. It will help keep you on course and make sure you never miss two days in a row.

Continue with the habit train: Once you have finished with the new habit, the goal is to get back to your normal routine or habit train as quickly as possible. If you do not get back to your previously established habits there is a chance that the habit train might derail. Hence, make sure an old/established habit follows the new habit. This way you have not created a big dramatic change to your routine. It is a subtle, almost surgical cut, to the established routine. Remember, the goal when creating your system is that it should not cause too much of a disruption in your current life. If there is a big disruption to your routine or life, the chances of the new habit sticking are much lower.

Review and improve: This is the most important part of a system. Once you start creating habits, you must review them from time to time. Review new habits on a daily basis. Review established habits once in a while, maybe once a week or once in two weeks.

The purpose of the review is to check if the habit is stickable. Have you been able to maintain it, or is it too much for your system?

The second thing to review is its impact. Is the habit serving you? Is the habit good for you?

You need to do this for both new habits as well as established habits. After a while the new habit will need to be tweaked and improved for one of two reasons:

1. If the habit you created is difficult to stick to, it means there is too much friction. Identify ways in which you can make it easier to do.
2. The habit might have been too easy for you if you started a reading habit and set a goal of two pages. This might become extremely easy in a weeks' time. You want to increase the pages to four pages a day. In this way, improve and grow your habit.

Remember habits aren't static things, they grow and change and improve with you! I explain this in detail in the next section.

System and Habits

We often make the mistake of trying to create a habit in isolation. These kind of 'isolated habits' fail. We have to make habits a part of a system. This way the old habits help in forming the new habits.

Making systems for your day is one of the best things you can do. A consciously designed system can change the energy you bring to your day. It can help you improve your relationships at home and at work. It can dramatically improve your health. Whatever change you want to make in your life, starts with a small habit. A small tweak to the life you are already living. Remember your motivation will fail. Your self-discipline will fail. But your systems will work!

Exercise

This is the most important step to tie in all the learnings from this book. On a fresh page in your notebook, write down the following for each of your new goals/habits:

1. *What do you want to change?*
2. *Intention*
3. *Habit Train or cue*
4. *New habit*
5. *Continue the Habit Train*
6. *Review and improve*

Sustaining Habits

15
The Stumbles and the Falls

I was about ten years old and had a pillow strapped to my back, held in place by my father's old adjustable leather belt. On days when I felt particularly vulnerable, I had another pillow strapped to my mid-riff. I was learning to skate.

I had those old skates that strapped onto one's shoes, held in place by buckles that always managed to pinch me. Scared and wide-eyed, I would hold on to the table and walls. Bending forward, bending backward. Trying my best to stay on those damn skates. When suddenly, out of nowhere there would be frantic movement, the skates would make this horrible sound of wheels screeching, and spinning and thud. I'd be looking at the ceiling, lying flat on my back, the wheel on my skate still spinning as I lay there motionless. Taunting me. Getting up was another dance altogether. Put pressure on one leg and the skate would slide off. Put pressure on the other and, thud! This time I'd land on my knee.

My parents in all their wisdom had taught me to protect myself with the pillow strapped to my bum. They knew that falling was going to be a part of the process. They knew that not getting hurt while falling down was just as important as the process of learning how to skate. The first few times I landed flat on my back; my parents rushed over to help. Then encouraged me back on my feet. After that, they made it normal. No more rushing to my aid, just a smile and a nod saying get up.

Falling and failing is hard. We need to be compassionate about the process.

One fine day, I put on my skates and left the pillow to the side, dad's leather belt went back into his wardrobe. I was confident of my abilities now. I knew where all the bumps and cracks were on the floor of my house, the places where I had tripped and fallen. I knew how to save myself in case I slipped. It all became second nature to me. I'd wake up in the morning, put on the skates and eat breakfast, lunch, and dinner with them on my feet. Zoom around the house with a glass of milk in my hand. I was Rockin' and Rollin'!

Failing is an important part of the habit-forming process as well. Whenever we do something completely new or when something stretches our comfort zone, failing should be built into the process. As children, we knew that failing went hand in hand with learning something new. Children don't get frustrated when they fall or fail at something. They just try again. But as adults we have this belief that we are now superior. That we should be able to get things perfect in the first round of doing it, that we know better and hence should be able to do everything easily.

Failure is seen as something bad. Something that must be avoided at all costs. This is because as adults we see failure as defeats. Everything is a competition and hence failure is a defeat. Defeats affect us psychologically. They make us feel less than the people around us. They play havoc with our self-image. We become the losers. The ones nobody wants to be with.

Children, on the other hand, unknowingly see failures as teachers. They learn from their failures and hence learn how to 'not fail' faster. Just like in my skating story, I slowly learned how to keep my balance. Trying this way and that to stay on the skate, till I found something that worked. If we don't keep trying, how will we find something that will ultimately work for us?

Clearly, children are wiser than us, we need to learn their attitude to see failure as a teacher.

Ask yourself:

1. What made me fail?
2. Where did I slip?
3. What can I do about it next time?

Notice there was no 'why' question. For most of us asking a 'why' question makes us doubt ourselves. It puts us in a downward spiral of self-judgment and self-flagellation. For instance, in response to 'Why did I not exercise today?', most of us would reply, 'Because I am lazy, because I have never been good at sticking to things, hence I will never be able to exercise as everyone else does.' Notice the negative spiral?

Now let's ask these questions again, replacing our opinions about ourselves, with facts.

'Why did I not exercise today?'

'I ran out of time because I woke up late.'

'Why did I slip?'

'I didn't manage my time well. Time management.'

'Why didn't I mange my time well?'

'I watched a show all the way to the end of its last episode because it was interesting.'

'So, how do I ensure I exercise tomorrow?'

Solution: 'I will not watch more than one episode of a show and will go to sleep thirty minutes earlier than I normally do.'

Notice the problem-solution approach? See the difference between the questioning process?

As adults, we ask too many 'whys' when things don't work out. Instead, we should ask 'why' while forming our intention.

As soon as we use the word 'why' we subconsciously believe that we have to justify our actions. This turns into a blame game. Instead, we need to show compassion for our failures. They are our teachers. The learning takes place by figuring out what we can do next, and not from beating ourselves up for failing. This is the key. The stumbles and falls can come from mistakes we make, which we learn from. The stumbles and falls can also come from the environment around us. Like when I was learning to skate, there used to be this hole in the middle of the bedroom floor. Quite a few times the wheel of my skate got trapped in that hole and threw me over face flat on the floor. There were also some tiles that were not in line. They tripped me every time I went over them, especially when I was learning. These kinds of environmental factors have to be dealt with in two ways, you either avoid them or learn to overcome them.

Imagine you are practicing the habit of quitting smoking. You realize every time you go to the club or pub you end up smoking. That is an environmental factor. You can try to avoid the club or pub till the non-smoking habit is firmly rooted. Instead, you can go to another kind of restaurant where smoking is difficult.

There are other environmental factors you cannot avoid like your best friends that order desserts after every meal. This was something I had to learn to deal with. When I was giving up sugar, I used to get so tempted by the desserts displayed in restaurants. I would go drool over them and then feel deprived. I soon learned to look the other way as I passed them on the way to my table. However, what I could not avoid looking at were the desserts my friends ordered at the table. And their 'mmmm' and 'ooooh' and 'aaaaaah' as they relished each bite. Earlier I used to excuse myself and use the washroom hoping they had finished. Then I learned to order an after-dinner tea to have along with them.

There were slip-ups of course. Days where I gladly offered my services to finish half the pastry. But I learned from these slip-ups too. Look at all the obstacles in your environment that are preventing you from sustaining a habit. Figure out how you can overcome them.

More importantly when you do fall or fail at the habit, how do you protect yourself? You have to plan for the failures. You have to have a pillow strapped to your back. These are the things that make the slip-ups less painful and allow you to bounce back stronger than ever!

At home, there were days I just craved for something sweet and would go mad trying to find something. I kept a few apricots and dates handy. They curbed my craving. They were not there to be had every day. Just on those days when I slipped. The goal was still to retreat from sweet.

Another example of a protection is creating a buffer. This is something I make all my clients do. Especially those who have to submit reports at work. I make them 'pre-crastinate' in place of procrastinating. 'Pre-crastinate' means to start working on a project as soon as they get it, so that in case procrastination sets in later, they have enough of a buffer. I use 'pre-crastination' while writing this book as well; trying to finish way before I need to submit anything.

I like to workout in the morning because I get it over and done with right in the beginning of the day. This way, if for some reason I cannot do it in the morning, I still have the evening to exercise. That is my pillow, my protection. If you have a habit of exercising in the evening, you lose that opportunity of protection from failure.

Find ingenious ways to protect yourself from falling and failing. Protect yourself from a small slip-up turning into a big bad fall.

I often speak to people who tell me that they are fed up of starting again and again. They say they have tried to maintain consistency but they fail each time. The obvious response to this is, they are failing because they are not learning from their mistakes. They are possibly making the same mistakes over and over again.

The biggest mistake of course is to rely on motivation, and not habits, to make a change.

I don't want you to blindly start again every time you fall off the habit. Instead I want you to:

- Dust yourself off
- Say 'it's okay'
- Ask yourself what you learned from this fall

And *only then* get back on to the habit.

Failing and falling are part of the process. The more comfortable you are with it, the faster you will grow. The faster you will change into the person you want to become.

16

Tracking Your Habits

I wasn't a very good student. I loved to learn but not to study. Curious by nature, I would have loved to know more about the folk that peopled my History books, but memorizing dates and places was absolute anathema; ditto exams. Passing was a cause for celebration at home, failing was a common occurrence. Yet I still remember most of what I learned, because I was curious about it! Getting my homework done was another nightmare for my parents. I would cry, scream, sulk, hide my books, do anything to get out of it. The next day a routine yelling by my teachers followed, while they fished out a red pen from their handbag and wrote a 'Bad Remark' in my diary for my parents edification and for them to sign-off on.

There was one teacher though, who would put up all the kid's names on a chart paper and draw a grid with the days of the week on the top. For every homework assignment submitted we would get a golden star. She spoke to us about the golden star and embellished it with meaning and praise.

Then one day I finished my homework and got a star. Every day that week I would go to that class and see that star. The next week it was gone. I had to get that star back. I worked on my homework and got another star. Then the next day I did the same! I now had two stars! Oh my God! The Excitement! I thought, let me see if I can get more. This was the only class I ever finished my homework for.

I was excited to do something so drab and boring only because I could see my progress visually, and those golden stars were so beautiful.

This is the power of tracking your habits and giving meaning to your tracking method. Tracking can be one of the most boring activities you do. Till you give it meaning and make it relevant to you. As a child that golden star looked so beautiful. It had a deep meaning for me.

It's easy to mistake that golden star as a reward. Most teachers give golden stars as a reward for the best homework submitted or some outstanding work.

This golden star was given to every kid who did their homework. It wasn't a reward. It was my first exposure to habit tracking!

Why Tracking Habits is Important

I believe that you cannot see progress looking forward. You can only see progress looking backwards. You have to see the journey to understand where you started and where you have reached.

The human brain normalizes things very quickly. A habit that you struggled with in the beginning becomes normal and then you forget that you are doing it. Which is the stage we want to reach. However, to get there you need to see progress. And the best way to see progress is by tracking your habits. Tracking habits does multiple things:

1. Reminds you of the habits you have to practice.
2. Shows you if you practiced it the day before or not.
3. Makes you aware if you are missing two days in a row.
4. Gives you a list of all the habits you are focused on practicing, at a glance.
5. Makes you feel great ticking-off a habit that has been completed for the day.

For many that last point is the most important. There is a great feeling of accomplishment when you tick off a habit you had planned. It rewires your brain to do more. I always like to make a song and dance about it. Every time I tick off a habit is like a mini celebration!

When you look at your habit list in the morning it gives you a feeling of excitement and anticipation. If you have chosen habits that are in line with your intentions, you should be excited to jump in and tick them off. Hence, tracking your habits becomes one of the cornerstones in creating practical habits.

Should you track habits on a daily, weekly, monthly basis? The duration you track a habit for, plays an important role in the way your tracker works. The purpose of tracking for a set duration is so that you can review your progress and make appropriate course corrections. These course corrections help you stay on track and focused.

How to Track Habits

Daily, weekly or monthly? Some experts suggest only focusing on each day and tracking a habit daily and reviewing the day you did the habit. But that duration is too small and you cannot see your momentum building up. Others believe that you should track your habits by the months. However, thirty-one days will have lots of ups and downs. If you review the progress only after a month, then too much time has passed. There are lots of calendars available that make you shade out a square for each day you did the habit across a month. They look very cool but are not practical.

The goldilocks zone is about a week. Seven days of tracking is just long enough to see a trend and just short enough to make corrective changes to the habit if needed. Another reason to use seven days is that there is no Mid-Point. You have either done the habit for four days that week, which is more than 50 per cent of the time; or if you did it for three days, then it is less than 50 per cent of the time. Remember, to form a habit, we need to do it for more than 50 per cent of the time. So, tracking per week is the best way to maintain a record of the way your habits are progressing.

Ideal number of times to practice the habit: The next thing we have to do is give ourselves a target or an ideal count for the number of times we are going to practice a particular habit. This is important. A football player needs a goal. Similarly, for tracking habits, we need an ideal count of the number of times we will do a habit. This will be a minimum count. You can exceed the count but try not to underachieve it. If 'week on week' you hit your ideal count, this is the key to consistency.

When setting up the ideal number of times you want to practice it per week, there are a few things to keep in mind.

1. Don't be over-ambitious and keep the ideal count at seven. Allow for mistakes and slip-ups.
2. Don't keep your ideal count at three days or less either. That means you are breaking the third rule of habit change, which is 'never miss two days in a row'.
3. Four is a good number for absolutely new habits. You can of course exceed it. But try not to go below it. Practicing a habit four times a week is a good idea.
4. For habits that you do multiple times a day (drinking water, Pomodoro, micro workouts) come up with a total number for the day and make that number the habit you track. Hence, the drinking water habit would be 'drink 3 litres of water daily'.
5. Try not to take Saturday and Sunday off. One, this again violates the 'never miss two days in a row' golden rule; and two, it becomes hard to get back on track on Monday!

These are tips that I learned through trial and error while working with my clients. So, they work in real-life scenarios. Focus on them. They are practical.

Once you have your ideal count then you can compare it to your actual count at the end of the week. See how well you have done. Did you over-perform? Give yourself a big '+' next to it. Did you underperform? Write a '-' next to it. And an '='

for hitting your target! This becomes a quick reference guide to how the week was. The more + and = signs, the better!

Describing the habit: When tracking a habit, make sure you describe what that habit will look like, in detail. This will help you maintain the habit and visualize completing it. Unfortunately, many people just write the habit as: drink water, yoga, work on the project, sleep, wake up at 5 a.m., etc. These kinds of descriptions do not place the habit in its context. As a result, the habit can vary from day to day. Our minds are always looking for a shortcut or a way to cheat on the things that require effort.

- For example, a drinking water habit will have a description like: 'Through the day I will drink and refill this 1-liter bottle three times'. This way there is no ambiguity, your green tea and juice are not part of your water habit. A morning yoga habit might have the description, 'At 7 a.m. after writing in my gratitude journal I will unroll and sit on the yoga mat' (using first Golden Rule 'Keep it stupidly small'). Working on a particular project habit might have a description like, 'I will complete six Pomodoro timers (25 minutes) working on this project.' Or, 'I will write a minimum of 500 words today.'

The description is vital, so when planning your habit, make it small enough and detailed enough. This way you will have carefully thought through the process of the habit and hence will be able to perform the action well.

The habit before and the habit after: The next important step, when designing a habit to track, is to insert it into a routine you already have. This way you do not create too much change and turmoil in your life. When you sneak a habit into an already established routine it is easier to solidify that habit into the routine. For example, most of us have a morning routine that might include tea or coffee. You could put a new habit immediately before or after the tea routine. I like doing my gratitude practice while drinking my coffee. As the coffee cools, I write my gratitude. Once I finish my coffee, I do my meditation. This way I have sandwiched the old habit with two new habits.

Don't make too many changes to an old routine or it will be difficult to follow.

So, when writing the description of the habit, mention what you will be doing before and after the new habit. 'I will make my coffee and as it cools write in my gratitude journal three new things that I am grateful for, after writing them I will drink my coffee.'

Notice how 'Making the coffee' is a habit and 'drinking the coffee' is another habit.

This way the gratitude habit has fit perfectly into the morning routine. Similarly, you could add exercise just before your morning bath. Or taking your vitamins and supplements immediately after food. Or an evening walk after dinner.

When tracking your habits always note what you will do before and after the habit as well.

How many habits to track: When you first start tracking your habits there will be a temptation to track everything that you do. This is just the initial excitement of tracking. However, if you do this, you will have a crowded habit tracker, the more crowded it is the less useful it will be.

I knew a person who got so excited that he added habits like breakfast, lunch, and dinner to his habit tracker. These were already very set routines for him. He ended up tracking twenty-five things every day. At some point he got fed up with it and just stopped tracking altogether claiming tracking was rubbish and just too much work.

The truth is that you need to have a very strict rule for the number of habits you track every day. Without this rule, it becomes an endless stream of habits. Habit tracking is a tool and has to be used in the right way. It is like using a screwdriver to shovel the ground. It will work, but is rubbish at it and just too much work!

So, the rules for how many habits to track are simple.

1. No more than three new habits.
2. No more than three old habits.

That is it, your list should have no more than six habits.

The new habits are those you have just introduced into your life. You are still uncertain about them. They have not perfectly set into your routine. There is still hesitation when it comes to them. The habit requires a reminder or some effort to complete. Or it is a habit you keep giving yourself an excuse for not doing. Tracking is especially important for new habits. However, any more than three new habits and your success rate drops fairly dramatically. This is because there is too much of a change in your routine. Hence it begins to fall apart.

A listener of *The Habit Coach* podcast once wrote to me, he had added ten new habits to his daily routines. He was struggling. He told me that every day was a fight. He would look at his habit list and feel overwhelmed. He felt that he did not have the ability to form new habits. The truth is, he had bitten off more than he could chew.

This reminds me of the old Indian story about trapping monkeys in a forest. All you have to do is keep a pot with a small mouth. Inside the pot keep lots of nuts. The monkey will put his hand in the pot and take a fist full, as many as it can hold. And when he tries to pull his hand out, it is stuck. The monkey does not realize that if he just takes one out, he will be free. He holds on to all of them and then wonders why he is stuck! So don't be a silly monkey.

Once a habit is firmly established and a part of your routine, move that habit into the Old Habit list. Keep tracking it for a while. Why must we track old habits? Well, only to make sure they don't disappear if we go on a holiday or something else happens in our life. We should ideally bounce back from a break like a holiday. The old habits help us in anchoring our routine back.

When to Stop Tracking Habits

There will come a time when you will need to stop tracking a habit because it is now firmly part of your routine or you have decided that this habit does not serve you and you want to drop it. The latter is easy, whenever you think a habit is no longer serving you, drop it. There are enough other new things that you can try to work on.

Once a habit becomes a part of your life you will know it. The habit is now automatic and requires almost no conscious effort or thought. It has become who you are. You have begun identifying yourself with it. For example, I stopped tracking my 'black coffee without sugar' habit when I realized that I no longer craved for a cappuccino or a milky coffee with sugar. I now considered myself a black coffee drinker.

I once had a client who had first fought me tooth and nail for not taking cold showers. She started it. In one of our meetings, I asked her how her cold shower habit was. She had to think and suddenly realized that her cold showers were now the default! She did not have to remember to do them anymore! When you reach this stage, you can stop tracking your habits.

The Hidden Habit

When you start tracking your habits you will learn that there is an important hidden habit that no one talks about, which is the habit of tracking the habits! If you don't put the tick marks against the habits, you will not be tracking them. Hence, one of the first habits to create is the habit of reviewing your day and ticking the habits.

There are two ways to form the habit of tracking. The first is to put a big tick mark as soon as you finish a habit. This itself acts as a reward or a good job for completing the habit.

The second way is to review your habits at night before bed. This way you have the whole day to catch any stray habits that did not happen at a designated time. This end-of-day review is easier to form as a habit, as it becomes a part of your night-time routine.

Play around with these two methods till you find one that works for you. It could also be a hybrid of these two. Some habits you tick mark immediately, while others you tick them off at night.

Make it a celebration: Whenever you tick mark a habit off your list for the day, make it a celebration. Either make a nice big tick mark and add a flourish to it. Or then say something to yourself to make you feel like a winner. Something like 'Yes, rock star!' or 'Good job' or 'You are on a roll'. Something to celebrate, something to make you feel good about yourself. This mini celebration when completing a habit is so important. It becomes something we look forward to the next day.

Tools for Tracking Habits

There are many ways you can track your habits. Here are a few of my favourites and most practical ways of doing it.

Using physical objects: I once had a client who was very proud of her wine cork collection. She would put all the corks in this huge glass bowl. One day, we were discussing how many glasses of alcohol she was allowed to have in a week. After some negotiation, we arrived at a number. A number that was lesser than what she was used to drinking each week.

We used the corks to set up her tracker. We filled one crystal bowl with the exact number of corks as the number of drinks she was allowed. Every time she had a drink, she would pick up one cork and put it back into the big collection. This way she could visually see her habit.

Another fun way of visually tracking a habit is by using paper clips. Find a hook or a nail near your desk or dressing table. Then place a bowl of paperclips next to it. Every time you do a particular habit, interlock a paper clip with the one hanging. This way you will form a chain. It is a great way of visually seeing a habit grow. At the end of a week or a particular timeframe, you can count the number of clips. Then the next time around you can start removing the clips one habit at a time, again seeing progress.

These visual cues are fun. If you are a creative person then this is a good way to enjoy the habit tracking process. The only issue with them is that you have no way of measuring if you missed two days in a row or not, as these are just a straightforward count.

You can use these visual cues to keep track of habits you do multiple times a day. For example, if you want to do micro workouts five times a day. Example: twenty squats, twenty push-ups, twenty jumping jacks, etc. A visual cue is a set of five blocks that I have near my desk. I just add one block on top of the other to form a tower. I aim to get all five blocks up and standing every day. (Hoping someone doesn't come and knock them over).

Writing it down: This is the classic way of tracking your habits. You can have a separate notebook for this or make it a part of your journal or gratitude journal.

There are many techniques you can use to track your habits on paper. The easiest is to write down the habits one below the other on the left. On the right side put the weekly count of the number of times you want to achieve the habit. Then every day just put a nice big tick mark next to it. On days you do not do the habit you can put an 'X' or a cross. This way you are aware of all the habits you have done and can keep a count of the missed days as well. Make sure you do not get two 'X's in a row. We do not want 'XX as this will violate the third Golden Rule of habit change.

If you want to spend more time on creating this habit-tracking journal you can draw vertical lines and make columns to represent days of the week: Monday to Sunday. Then leave an empty row to total the habits for the week and then continue Monday to Sunday. This way you can form a full grid!

If you love drawing, take the time to decorate your tracking pages. Make it a fun exercise to do. Don't think of it as tedious and extra work. Instead, think of it as a creative outlet. If you like, instead of putting tick marks for a completed habit, you can even put golden star stickers. Just like my favourite teacher in school did.

Spreadsheets: If you are someone who is used to tracking numbers and data for work or if you just enjoy your Excel sheets, this tracking method is for you. But if you are the kind of person who faints at the thought of opening up a spreadsheet, stay far far away! Especially, since you are going to have to open this sheet up every day to keep a track of your progress. If that is going to be difficult to do, do not use this method.

You can use programs like Excel or Google Sheets to track your habits. The advantage of this method is that you can track your numbers easily. Keep track of the weekly target and the actual habit without much fuss and calculation. If you are using Google Sheets you can even share the sheet with your Accountability Partner (discussed in detail in the next chapter) so that they can keep a check on your progress. The way to use a spreadsheet for tracking is to have the dates and days of the week on the first row. In the first column list your habit and the description of it. Then in the second column write the ideal weekly target for each habit.

Now after seven days leave a blank column. Here you can put a formula that automatically calculates the score for you.

Score = Actual repetitions - Ideal repetitions

This way, each week you will automatically know if you are up or down on your count that week.

When marking the habits, put a '1' for each day you completed the habit successfully. Put a '0' for days you were not able to. And leave that cell blank on days you were not supposed to do that habit. This way you will be able to catch yourself from making '00' or two misses one after another.

Use numbers on the spreadsheet, do not use X and O or any other letter. Numbers are easier to calculate scores with. Like I said, use this method only if you are very comfortable with spreadsheets. If not, this can soon become a daily nightmare.

Calendar on the wall: This is the simplest way to start your habit-tracking journey. We get desk calendars or wall calendars that have squares to write things in. Just write the habit you did that day on the calendar. This is the easiest way to begin. It is not as elegant as the other methods, but the advantage is that this calendar is in your face. You see it on the wall or on your desk. Hence it acts as a helpful reminder to do the habits you have planned.

Using an app: There are many different apps that exist in the market today. Each has its benefits and drawbacks. A few apps follow the habit-streak method of motivating you. As discussed earlier, these habit-streaks often have the exact opposite effect. They demotivate you if you miss the habit on a day. You feel like you have dropped the ball and just give up altogether.

The advantage of an app is that it stays with you in your pocket wherever you go. You can set alarms and reminders to complete a habit. It will automatically track and give you the statistics. There are different themes you can use to make the apps fun and interesting. Apps are a great all-round solution to tracking your habits.

Pro Tip 1: Keep the app icon on your main screen so you see it every day. It acts as a visual reminder to click on the app.

Pro Tip 2: Set a reminder on your phone to make sure you mark off the habits each day. This reminder should be at the end of every day.

Tracking habits needs to become a habit as well. It is one of the most important tools in your tool box to help with consistency. Tracking habits can become a pain, once the initial excitement wears off. So, make sure you have chosen a method that you find easy and interesting to do.

Exercise

Decide a tracking method for yourself. Which of the above methods made the most sense to you? This is a very personal and individual journey so choose a method that speaks to you.

Once you settle on a tracking method make sure you have easy access and can update the tracker easily.

17
Your Accountability Partner

I remember my paternal grandmother sitting me down as a child and telling me a story, probably because I must have fought with my cousins. I believe it was from *Aesop's Fables*. A father was fed-up with his four sons quarrelling with each other. When they were about to leave home and set up their lives independently, he told them to fetch him sticks and small branches, which they did. The father tied them all together and gave the bundle to each of the sons in turn, asking them to break it. They tried as hard as they could, but each failed.

The father then untied the knot that held the bundle together, gave each of them one stick and asked them to break it. SNAP, SNAP, SNAP, SNAP! Each of them broke the stick. He then told his sons that together they would be stronger and unbreakable, but more likely to break and fail if they were alone.

Now clearly my grandmother must have told me this story which such flair that it is still stuck in my head. The principles apply when it comes to fixing, setting and maintaining your habits. If you go on this journey of change and improving your habits by yourself, you will definitely make progress. But in order to cement these habits and to make sure that you do well on this journey, you need to involve others to help you.

We call these people accountability partners. These are the people who are our closest friends and family, or people we don't know well, or even complete strangers (as we will see).

The Role of an Accountability Partner

1. The person must have access to your habit tracker and check it regularly.
2. The person must be able to see the progress you are making and comment on it.
3. The person must know how to confront you when you are not practicing the habit as you had committed to.
4. The person must be able to encourage you when you just don't feel like it or have had a break.
5. The person must be like a cheerleader and celebrate your victories with you.

The accountability partner clearly plays different roles. Hence it is important for you to choose someone who can fulfil these roles. If you have someone who is unable to stand up to you and hold you accountable, then it is fairly useless. He is an accountability partner in name only.

It is also your responsibility to keep the accountability partner in the loop. Updating him about your habits and if you are doing them or not. This step is important too. As without information, the accountability partner will not be able to hold you accountable.

You can also choose to have different accountability partners for different habits. If there are habits you do at home, your partner or someone you stay with might make for a good accountability partner. If it is a habit at work, you might choose a co-worker to be your accountability partner.

Who Can Be Your Accountability Partner?

Friends, Family and co-workers: This category will form the largest chunk of your accountability partners. They know you the best and hence have the ability to encourage you or give you a 'whack' when you are not sticking to the habits. They are also your biggest cheerleaders and want you to succeed. Over the years I have seen many family members make good accountability partners. Especially if they have a good relationship with the person.

Some of the cutest and most vigilant accountability partners are your children. This is because children understand the concept of rules very well. 'Mumma you are not supposed to be doing this.' 'Daddy you said you are not going to do it, why are you doing it?' They are inquisitive by nature and have a sneaky way of sussing out things. They will keep you true to your goal with brutal honesty, they have no filter. So, if you have a child at home, involve them in your habit. Explain the habit to them and then watch them bug you to do it!

Friends also make for good accountability partners, especially if you are tracking each other's habits. A daily catch-up message to each other or a phone conversation is all you need to stay updated. So, look around and see among the people you know, who can be a good accountability partner for you.

People who you do not know well: These are people who you might meet at workshops or virtual events. You might be doing a study course together and hence have the same objectives. If you are a writer, there are many writing clubs you can join where the members of the club become each other's accountability partners. There is a set goal or habit they have and the members keep a tab on each other. You start off not knowing your accountability partner at all, they are strangers. But in the process, you might become good friends.

These kinds of accountability partners are interesting because as humans we always try to impress the people we do not know; try and create a good impression. While people we do know well, we tend to take for granted.

Strangers: Some of the best accountability partners are people who we do not know at all. We can harness the power of social media for good by making our followers on social media, our accountability partners. Put your habit and your goal out there. And then tell them you will be updating them daily on your progress. Then every time you do the task, take a picture and upload it.

You will be surprised that people will remember and hold you to it when you do not do it. At the same time, since you have made such a grand announcement, the chances of you sticking to it are higher. I used social media as my accountability partner when I did the no sugar challenge. Or started my habit of going for a walk every day. Or when I started having a salad every day.

If you have a body goal or a fitness goal, you can use social media to post progress pictures. Show everyone how the progress is taking place. Don't underestimate the power of strangers in being your accountability partners. When you have a good accountability partner, making changes to habits are easier. You are not alone in the process. You have someone holding your hand and keeping you honest with your goals and habits. Like the story, my grandmother told me. We are stronger together and individually we SNAP.

Exercise

Find yourself an accountability partner for each of the three habits you have decided to create for yourself.

You could have three different accountability partners, or just one for all three.

Be honest with your accountability partner/s, share your intention, share what you are going to be doing and the frequency with which they should check in on you.

Tell them what you expect from them clearly. Tell them how to hold you accountable.

18

The Power of Practice

I remember trying to hula hoop for the first time. I had seen videos of kids doing it. It looked so effortless, spinning that hoop around the waist. Smiling. Dancing along. How hard could it be?

Well, it took me two months before I could last for thirty seconds, spinning that hoop. The first time I tried, the hoop dropped to the ground without making one single turn. The next time, I tried shaking my body as if I was possessed and still nothing! The reason for wanting to learn to hula hoop was that I had just started a fitness class, where I was making fitness fun. I thought hula hoops would be a great addition to the process, little did I know how frustrating learning it would be.

My parents kept telling me about how they used to hula back in college and how easy it was. They kept giving me pointers. However, I soon learned that my technique was not right. Getting the right advice is so important.

> *'You can practice shooting 8 hours a day, but if your technique is wrong, then all you become is very good at shooting the wrong way. Get the fundamentals down and the level of everything you do will rise.'*
>
> *MICHAEL JORDAN*

I found some good tutorials on YouTube and started. I began to improve. However, progress was still slow. Nevertheless, I set aside time every day to practice. I put a hoop in my room and every time I saw the hoop I would go and practice.

Practice is very simply about getting the right kind of repetitions in. The more you repeat the ideal behaviours, the higher your chance of becoming good at what you do. Habits are all about practice, practice, practice. Repetition is the key to getting good at habits. You have to be willing to put in the time and practice in order to make habits permanent.

Have you noticed how you take a shower every day? You will always wash your body in the exact same way, use the same hand to soap or wash yourself. This is the power of practice. No matter how tired or sleepy you are. Your body will go through the same motions because they have been practiced so many times!

Within two months I was hooping and was able to keep the hula hoop on my hips for the duration of a song. Then I decided to go to a hula-hooping class. The instructor made us walk while the hula was rotating around our waist! I was back to square one. Dropped it so many times, it was embarrassing. Then she made us stand and clap our hands. The hula dropped again! My mind could not focus on so many tasks at the same time. I came home and practiced these new techniques.

While hula-hooping is a skill and not necessarily a habit, making a daily practice of it is. In just the same way, any habit that you choose to form needs that dedicated practice. I give the example of a skill because skills are very hard and very frustrating to practice and master.

As your Habit Coach, I want you to only focus on the repetition of that habit. Make each repetition count. Practice till it becomes second nature to you. For example, writing this book has turned into a habit for me. Every morning I wake up, make my coffee, meditate and then start writing the book. I work for two hours and finish about 1,000 words. This took repetition and practice until it became something I didn't have to think about or force myself to do anymore.

My favourite quote by Bruce Lee is, 'I don't fear the man who has practiced 10,000 kicks. I fear the man who practiced one kick 10,000 times'. Similarly, in order to make a positive shift in your life you have to keep improving yourself. Practicing that habit over and over till it becomes second nature.

You may know all the theories in the world. You may have access to all the best information. But if you do not put it to practice, if you do not act on it, if you do not make it a habit, it will never help you or change your life! So just like all the great athletes of the world who are the icons of practice, make yourself a practice schedule. You got to know what to practice when and keep track of it all.

Exercise

Now is when you start with your habits, if you have not already. No more excuses, no more waiting for Monday. It starts from today. The more you practice the habits, the more you stay consistent with them, the faster you will see the change.

Action is the most important part of the process. We can intellectually understand everything, but if we do not physically start, it is useless.

So get your system in place and get cracking!

19

The Power of Consistency

Have you heard of the man who carried a four-year-old bull on his shoulders, up a hill? To put things in perspective that is about 1,000 kg or about 2,200 pounds. Can you imagine that?

This is the story of a man who lived around 540 BCE. If you search online for Milo of Croton, you will be overwhelmed by the number of stories describing his unbelievable strength. As well as stories about what he ate every day—9 kg of meat, 9 kg of bread and 10 litres of wine.

Milo of Croton had won six Olympic titles. He was a wrestler and a soldier. As a party trick, he would tie a band around his head, breathe in, swell the veins in his forehead and break the band. However, what he is most famous for was how he became this strong. Legend has it that a baby bull was born on his farm. He lifted this calf on his shoulders and carried it around with him every day. He would carry it up the hill. He would carry it into town and through the market. He made it a habit of carrying that calf around with him.

Now, carrying a newborn calf on your shoulders is easy. It must have been fairly light at 40 kg. But as it grew it became heavier and Milo, carrying it up and down daily, grew stronger. When the calf turned a year old it would have weighed about 500 kg. That's not lightweight at all. At two years old, the bull would have been 725 kg. At year three, the bull would have been 860 kg. But by carrying the bull every day for four years, as the bull grew bigger, Milo grew stronger.

Three key takeaways from this story:

1. Patience (four years)
2. Kaizen (bull growing)
3. Compounding (Milo's strength growing too)

Patience: Habits and consistency work together to create superhuman results. Both use one critical raw material. Something that we believe we have too little of. That raw material is time. One of my favourite Lao Tzu quotes is, 'Nature does not hurry, yet everything is accomplished.' Isn't it beautiful? There is no hurry or sense of urgency. There is calm and consistency.

The society we live in today is centred around the belief that we do not have time. That time is constantly slipping away through our fingers and that we have to hold onto it as tightly as possible. We are socially being programmed to live in a world of immediate gratification. We don't have time to wait. And as we will see, immediate gratification is one of the signs of a 'bad habit'. We are constantly bombarded with 'get rich quick' schemes, 'lose 10 kgs in 1 week', 'spend now, pay later', etc. These ideas are so attractive that they draw us in.

When I was a kid, I had to wait a whole month for my parents to take me to the market to buy a toy. When Amazon first started, it would take a week or more to get what you bought. Then it got reduced to two days. Then next-day delivery and finally same-day delivery. These services are amazing and they improve our lives for sure. But they also completely destroy our patience. Remember the queues at banks, the walk or run to the landline to receive a call, and the slow internet of the 1990s?

The ability to stay calm when you have to wait a long time is patience. Patience is a key skill needed in order to be consistent. If you are impatient or lose interest in something quickly, you will never be able to grow with it! You will start a new habit and, in a few weeks, lose interest. You will start a nutrition plan, not see any results in two weeks and will stop.

I know so many people who have a library filled with half-read books, a life filled with half-finished projects and bedrooms with half-cleaned wardrobes. This inability to stick with something, is because we keep finding something else more exciting. The 'grass is greener on the other side' syndrome. As your Habit Coach, I want you to learn the art of patience.

Here are three truths about patience:

1. **No amount of restlessness will make the time go faster.** You cannot speed up time. Just because you want it to, it won't flow faster. If you have an hour-long wait, it will last one hour. The best place to learn this is at an airport terminal. Ever seen the reaction on the faces of people whose flight has been delayed by an hour? They are grumpy, restless and fretting. Being grumpy will not make that flight arrive any faster. It will just make the

hour-long wait feel like a two-hour wait. Understand that time ... will take its own sweet time!

2. **Some things will take the exact amount of time they need and there is nothing you can do about it.** You can't plant the seeds of a rose bush today and expect roses tomorrow. Yet that is how we behave when it comes to our lives. We want to lose 10 kg in five days, not realizing it took us a few years to put on the 10 kg in the first place! It will take its own time.
3. **The trick to patience is enjoying this moment, not worrying about the next.** We are so focused on the outcome that we forget to enjoy the moment. We are like a kid on a road trip asking 'are we there yet, are we there yet?' Instead, imagine if we were singing and joking and playing games on that road trip. Time would fly by. The truth is, focus on the choices you make this instant. They are the only things that count!

But patience alone will not give you the result you want. You now have to learn how to use the time to your advantage. You can't be patient and do nothing. You will just stay the same. You have to be patient and plant the seeds of growth. This is where the concept of Kaizen comes in.

> *'Patience is not the ability to wait but the ability to keep a good attitude while waiting.'*
> JOYCE MEYER

Remember Milo and the bull? It took Milo four years to attain that incredible strength. It was not something that he attempted to achieve overnight. It wasn't a twenty-one-day challenge to lift a four-year-old bull. It took time and Milo showed patience.

Kaizen: The Japanese principle of 'continuous small changes' or 'continuous improvement' is called Kaizen. This one principle helped catapult Japan to an economic force after the destruction of World War II. The idea originated in the manufacturing process of factories. Industries were transformed and their efficiency went through the roof!

The concept is simple. Keep looking for small ways to improve the manufacturing process. It can be at all stages of the process. You can improve the quality of the materials used, the time taken for a task, the process of sorting and storing. Basically, any aspect of the way work is done. The power of kaizen lies not in making big dramatic changes, but in the small tiny changes that add up and together feel like a big dramatic change.

For example, a small change—having colour coded buckets for various raw materials—saved time that used to be spent in reading the small labels stuck on each bucket earlier. It doesn't sound like much, but saving 30 seconds, 8 times a day equals 4 minutes. Four minutes over 365 days equals 1460 minutes. Which is equal to 24 hours! It freed up almost one full day of work! Imagine hundreds of such small changes taking place all over a factory!

Such is the power of Kaizen, or continuous improvement through continuous small changes. Kaizen is especially important when it comes to our habits.

A mistake we often make is that we plan a habit and then just keep doing that same habit over and over and over again. We don't make a change to it. Hence, it never grows. As a result, our growth is slowed down as well. I used to see this lady at the gym. She would come and walk on the treadmill every day for an hour at the same speed. Full marks for consistency, however, she was not improving. Her body and health were stuck at that same pace. Maybe her diet needed a change, or some other area was not being addressed. Using kaizen would have helped her look for small changes that might have helped accelerate the change needed.

Many of us find ourselves on this exact treadmill of life. One day exactly like the last. It is a boring existence. The same job, same five dishes repeated over and over again, same TV serial night after night. These are all habits we are stuck in. The habits have not grown. Hence, we have not grown. We are only as good as our habits because our habits form our life! So as the habits improve, so do we.

I was once working with this young boy who suffered from a very extreme form of depression. He had been referred to me by his psychiatrist. He hated his life and wanted to end it. There was a sense of hopelessness. He just could not visualize his life improving. He felt stuck. And to be honest, he was stuck. His life was in a rut. One day we were talking and I told him something that completely changed his outlook. I told him, 'We are not looking for a miracle to change your life. We are only looking at making each day just 1 per cent better.' His eyes lit up, 'This I can do', he said.

Ever since then, his mantra became 'just 1 per cent better'. He kept looking for things that he could change in his life, just 1 per cent at a time! This gave him hope that tomorrow would be better than today.

In the same way, look at the habits that you are creating. Look at your current habits as well. Then every time you repeat them, think about how you could make them just 1 per cent better! What tiny thing could you improve on in the process?

A daily habit as common as brushing your teeth can be improved by changing the toothpaste or the toothbrush, using up and down strokes instead of circular strokes, brushing for longer, alternating both hands to brush your teeth, you could try tongue scraping after brushing. There is always room for improvement. Nothing dramatic. Just one tiny change at a time.

Here are a few questions you can ask yourself to come up with kaizen ideas for your daily habits:

- Can I reduce the amount of time needed for this activity?
- Can I make it easier to do the activity, where is the friction now?
- Can I find a less expensive alternative?
- How can I make this more challenging so it fuels my growth?
- Who can help me with this habit?
- Is there a better habit I can do instead?
- If I do this activity at another time of day, will it make things better?
- How can I make this habit measurable so I can track it?
- Can I change the location where I do the activity?
- Can I change the location of the tools I need for this activity?
- How can I change my mindset for this activity?
- Can I change the tools needed for the activity?

Every time you do the habit, see how you can make it better. The key aspects of change can be location, time of day and tools used.

Location as an example: My client would sit on the sofa and work on her laptop. I made a small shift to her working schedule. We designated a specific place on her dining table as her desk. This made her more focused when working, it also got rid of her back pain from sitting on the soft sofa all day. One small change in location made a difference to the habit.

Time as an example: A client of mine found that his days were pretty full with work. He would wake up at 6 a.m. to exercise. However, 6 a.m. was also when he had the most peace for his creative work. We shuffled the time around, instead of exercising at 6 a.m., now he would do his creative work at that time. Exercise was moved to 4:30 p.m., which was usually a time of low productivity and snacking. A simple change in time created a ripple effect of benefits.

Tools as an example: I started *The Habit Coach* podcast around 2019. We have three episodes every week. And I like to script out and work on these episodes. When I started the podcast, it used to take me about three hours to work on a script. Then I created a template for the script, where I could plug in my ideas and hence help plan the podcast better. This simple tool reduced my writing time by about half. Now, writing a podcast script takes me anywhere from forty-five minutes to an hour. Using tools can dramatically help your habits and make them more powerful or efficient.

Remember Milo and the bull? The bull getting older and heavier was the principle of Kaizen at play. It was a continuous improvement to the weight Milo had to carry. In Milo's case, it was a system that improved itself. A small change in the habit can have a magnified effect on your life. This is where the magic of compounding comes into play.

Compounding: While Kaizen is the improvement that takes place in the actual habit or action or thought process, the magic of compounding takes place in you as a person and in your life. It is that accumulation of all the small actions you take towards your goal that build up over time into something huge! To put things in perspective, if we follow the 1 per cent better each day as a rule due to the power of compounding our lives would improve by thirty-six times in the first year! For instance, if we start at 100 (I know it is difficult to quantify) then 1 per cent every day compounded would equal 3,778.34. That is a change from 100 to 3,778.34!

Let me explain this as a real-life example, without numbers.

My parent's favourite story about me as a baby was that I never walked. I didn't go through the walking phase that most babies go through. I apparently went from rolling on the floor, to crawling, to standing up and wobbling. Then one fine day I just started running around the house. This is a perfect example of compounding.

Every day a baby tries to move, tries to stand. This is a habit being formed. The muscles are getting stronger, sense of balance is improving, motor skills are improving as well. At this point, so many parents start to compare their baby's progress to others and panic because their baby is still not walking. The child has been continuously getting better and better, but the progress is so small and tiny that each small achievement is not noticeable. Then one fine day it all changes! The total impact of the habit is felt. The baby is walking. Blink and you will miss their first steps! This is the magic of compounding.

Compounding is the accumulation of these little efforts and the repetition of the habit that ultimately changes you. Nothing dramatic will happen in the first week or month of practicing a habit. Remember we start all our habits stupidly small. They grow with us over time, as mine have. People look at my life and joke that they could never be as 'hardcore' as I am about the various aspects of my life that I value. Like my health, my work, my relationships, and my service to others. They don't understand how I manage to do so much in one day.

This is the beauty of compounding; my life was nothing like this a few years ago. It took over six years to develop. Slowly, my habits were shaping my life. Their effect compounded into the person you see before you now.

When you see an entrepreneur running multiple businesses, you are inspired and wonder how they must be doing it. You see, for them running multiple businesses is much easier compared to you starting your first business. Their business management skills have compounded over time. They have grown so substantially over the years that it is easy for them.

The same thing exists when we see professional athletes. They have repeated the same habits for so long that their abilities have compounded over time. Their extraordinary abilities are nothing more than habits practiced like crazy! It is not easy to do. But it is possible. Compounding has made them superhuman!

Remember Milo and the bull? The ability to carry 1,000 kg on his back grew slowly as his strength compounded over time. It did not happen overnight. Consistent action over a period of time compounded into the insane strength that made him a legend.

20

Challenges: Stretching Your Comfort Zone to Form a Habit

Now that you have started on your habit journey, it's time to stretch your comfort zone a bit more and learn to sustain these habits. As you progress in your habit journey, you slowly need to expand your comfort zone to keep the journey both interesting and sustainable. Let me explain this with my own example. I was a year into my own personal fitness journey. I had started exercising regularly, five times a week. I watched what I ate and did intermittent fasting. Things were going smoothly, when a friend shared her own experience and I decided to take on that challenge too. It really stretched my comfort zone!

She shared that a friend was addicted to cola and drank about 3 litres of cola a day and to get over this habit had started a 100-day no-sugar challenge. I had never heard of it before but it sounded scary. I could not imagine not having sugar for 100 days. I sat in disbelief for a while, thought about it and then told my friend that I was going to do it as well. In support of the person trying to break her habit, I thought that there was nothing better than a total stranger supporting her and doing it along with her.

So, I marked the 100 days out on my calendar and noticed that there were birthdays and festivals in there. I thought about all the cakes and sweets I would be missing out on. But with pure willpower, grit, determination and stupidity, I decided that I would not consume anything that had sugar in it. So, no sugar in my tea or coffee, no desserts, biscuits, cakes, and no chocolates for sure.

Then I realized that my everyday foods had sugar in them as well. There is sugar in bread, ketchup, salad dressings, and beer! To add insult to injury a new brewery had just opened up nearby. How the hell was I going to survive this? It was a journey of self-discovery. I learned all the ways my mind knew how to bargain and cheat. I learned that addictive substances will come and address you in your dreams. I had nights where I would dream of eating cakes and desserts. A friend of mine who did this challenge with me the next year, had a dream that she was being chased by a rolling donut!

Addictive substances like sugar need to leave your bloodstream.

The first month was hard! Thirty-five days into the challenge and I was learning just how much was not allowed. Every time I went to a restaurant I had to ask if the sauce had sugar in it. I started making tomato ketchup at home. The next thirty-five days were slightly less challenging because the draw towards sugary things had left me. I no longer craved them. Towards the end of the challenge, it had become so ingrained in me that I had forgotten when the challenge was going to end!

When I looked at myself in the mirror, I of course had lost quite a bit of fat. But more interestingly, my skin had cleared up completely. The dark patches on my skin had disappeared. Those tiny annoying bumpy pimples had disappeared. My energy was stable throughout the day. I genuinely was a different person.

Probably on day 110 I decided to break the no sugar challenge with my favourite donut. I took one bite into it. My head exploded. My skin began to crawl. It was just so ridiculously sweet! Something I had never noticed before. If anything, I used to believe that it wasn't sweet enough. That's when I realized just what an impact sugar had had in my life.

After completing the challenge I decided to change my habits. I made sure no chocolate or desserts came home to tempt me in the late evenings. I did not add sugar to my tea or coffee ever again. It's been six years now. Sliced bread that contains sugar is again completely out of my list of foods that I eat. Flavoured, sweetened sodas were replaced with plain sodas. I had apricots and figs at arm's reach, in case I wanted to pacify my sweet desires.

Ketchup, which used to be an everyday condiment, left my house forever. If you come home and want ketchup with your chips, we would have to order it from the store for you. Earlier, I used to go through a ketchup bottle every two weeks. I used to layer it on my fried eggs, chicken, burgers and even my dal and rice. It made anything taste good. Well, probably because it is about 50 per cent sugar! I replaced the ketchup with mustard, Togarashi, Tabasco and other interesting condiments that had no sugar.

These habits that I have maintained for all these years exist in me only because I took that giant leap of starting a challenge. If I had not done a challenge, I would not have been able to experiment and break out of my comfort zone.

Nowadays people use the word challenge very loosely. They call it a twenty-one-day exercise challenge to form a habit. That's not what the role of a challenge is. Challenges are not habits and habits are not challenges. You have to approach them differently.

Challenges and Habits: Key Differences

1. **Challenges are for a defined period of time, while habits are for life or till they stop adding value to your life:** This is why I believe that dieting is a form of challenge. Because it has a defined timeframe, you can only diet for a set number of days. If you make a dietary change that is going to last for the rest of your life (as I did by the end of my 100-day no-sugar challenge), you are no longer 'dieting', it has become your new normal.
2. **Challenges require a lot of willpower, motivation and grit, habits do not:** The goal of habits is to make them as easy and peaceful to implement as possible. The goal with a challenge is to make them as 'challenging' to implement as possible.
3. **Challenges break your comfort zone, while Habits stretch your comfort zone:** The challenge is designed to make your life uncomfortable so that you can learn fast and experience that change—however, as humans we can only be uncomfortable for a set amount of time. A habit, on the other hand, is designed to slowly grow the comfort

zone by stretching it. Hence habits are longer lasting as an impact.

As your Habit Coach, I want you to never mistake the two again.

- Use challenges to dramatically shake-up your life.
- Use habits to permanently change your life.

Hence, writing in your gratitude journal is not a challenge. It is something that you should make a habit of.

How to Use Challenges

Use challenges when you want to break an addiction: For example, if you have been having a drink every night and want to stop it, challenge yourself to not have a drink for fourteen days. This will show you what daily challenges you will face when you eventually try to quit it as a habit, i.e., quit it for good.

Use challenges to break an excuse you have been telling yourself or learn a new skill: For example, if you want to improve the way you write, challenge yourself to write 500 words every day for a month. I used this very successfully to get my blog off the ground. Initially, I kept procrastinating, but once I decided it was a challenge, I just dove right in. Or challenge yourself if you want to improve your cooking skills, by deciding to cook yourself one meal a day for fifteen days. This way you get to practice and learn new recipes. However, if you do not wish to continue cooking for yourself, you can always stop after the challenge.

Use challenges to create a dramatic change or a new foundation for future habits: I used to do a challenge where I did ten pull-ups every day of the first week. Then twenty pull-ups every day of the second week and thirty pull-ups every day of the third week. This simple challenge made me so strong in my pull-ups that I could transition to tougher exercises after that!

Use challenges to build a community and a support system: I have used the no-sugar challenge over the years to create a community. Thousands of people have been a part of various no-sugar challenges along with me. I have also joined challenges after passing through a difficult phase in my life. The feeling of community, when taking up a challenge together, is a great psychological booster.

Hence, feel free to indulge in as many challenges as you like, they are great teachers. They often show us our true colours! However, never, ever, ever mistake a challenge for a habit. They are totally different things and have different roles in our lives.

21

Habits Are Not about the Goal Alone, Habits Are about the Journey

How long does it take to form a habit is one of the first questions I am asked when I tell someone that I am a Habit Coach. This is because of two main reasons. The first is that we are so destination-oriented. We feel that establishing a habit is the goal. This goal orientation is what causes us to miss the bigger picture. It is like taking the family on a road trip, and all the while the kids in the back seat are jumping up and down asking, 'Are we there yet?' You just want to tell them to sit back, shut up and look out the window at the palm trees going past. In the same way, habits are not about the goal alone, as I have explained earlier. Habits are about the journey. A good, well-established habit will be your constant companion for the rest of your life! So, there is no real 'end goal' in mind. Especially since the habit will change and morph and evolve with you over time.

Hence, the first thing all of us need to do is to stop thinking about habits as a 'final destination'. Instead, we need to think about habits as steps on a journey. Each step moves us a little more forward along the path of life. I know of so many stories of people who believed that if they had not 'established a habit' they had failed. When they believed that they had failed, they stopped trying altogether. They gave up on creating that habit saying, 'I can't do it'. What a waste. Only because our idea of what a habit is, is wrong.

The second reason for this 'how long does it take to form a habit' question, comes from the famous twenty-one-day rule. That 'it takes twenty-one days to form a habit'. However, there are a few glaring flaws with this way of thinking. Let's first understand where this notion of twenty-one days to form a habit came from. It came from Dr Maxwell Maltz, a plastic surgeon in the 1950s, who observed that it took at least twenty-one days for his patients to get used to the surgery that had been performed. For example, if he had worked on someone's nose, it took them at least twenty-one days to get used to it; or, if he had to amputate a limb, the Phantom Limb syndrome would last for at least twenty-one days. He described this 'minimum of twenty-one days' as a phenomenon for the old mental image to dissolve and a new image to be formed.

This observation by Dr Maltz kept getting quoted all over the place and with each passing share, the meaning of the phrase changed and 'mental image' changed into 'a habit'. This idea was further developed and reinforced in a few self-help books later.

In 1960 Dr Maxwell Maltz published a book called *Psycho-Cybernetics*.[1] It was a fascinating book on behaviour change. It sold millions of copies worldwide and has influenced countless writers, self-help gurus, and motivational speakers.

In this book, he talks about experiences his patients had and also mentions his own life experiences.

You see this 'twenty-one days' number, in today's world obsessed with numbers and goal-oriented behaviour, is just another concept. It rolls off the tongue well. However, a lot of research has been conducted proving that there is no definite timeframe to form a habit—some studies say thirty days while others say sixty days.

Over the years as a Habit Coach, I have met so many people with this goal-oriented approach to forming a habit. The interesting problem is that once they pass the twenty-one-day mark they feel that the habit has been established and stop doing it! This is because they were just interested in the chase. Once the destination was reached, they just dropped the habit.

A listener of *The Habit Coach* podcast once wrote to me saying that she had tried so hard to form her reading habit. Slowly over time, she was able to spend an hour reading each day. Which was her goal. Once she had successfully done this for a month she ditched the habit altogether and looked for the next thing that she could do.

In truth, it is the journey that is most enjoyable, not the destination. This is something that I learned while trekking in the Himalayas. As a newbie trekker, you are so focused on getting to the next campsite. While all the experienced trekkers amble along, sit on rocks, look out at the scenery, laugh, joke, sing songs. My first trek was to Mt. Everest Base camp. It was a 14-day journey. It remains one of the most beautiful and life-changing experiences of mine to date. It taught me so much about myself, my limits and my mind.

The trek started off in this beautiful Rhododendron Forest. Bright red flowers everywhere. I barely noticed them. I walked as fast as I could so that I could reach the destination. I was so scared of getting tired or failing on the way that I rushed to the next stop for the night. That's when I heard my first Nepali words, 'bistari bistari', which translates to 'slowly slowly'. All the mountain guides would look at us walking with tremendous purpose and grit and determination. They would then flash this big white toothy smile and say 'bistari bistari'. The exact same intention is shared across mountain guides across the world. Trekking in Leh we heard the guides say 'Holé holé'. 'Slow slow'. When trekking in Africa while climbing Kilimanjaro the guides would say 'Polé Polé'.

That first night our trek leader, Samir Patham (or Sam in short) told us something very important. He said, 'you have come here all the way to enjoy the fresh air and the beautiful scenery. Don't worry, the campsite is not going anywhere. The mountain is not going anywhere.' This is the best way to think about your habits as well.

Look around and enjoy the journey of forming habits. Don't get obsessed with reaching the end.

The second thing I learned on the Everest basecamp trek was, what to do when the journey got hard. It was the fifth or sixth day of the trek. By now we were on higher ground, around 3,000 to 4,000 meters above sea level. Breathing was hard, if you sat down to tie your shoelaces and got up too quickly, you felt woozy. A constant dull headache became our companion.

We had started off at 7 a.m., had been trudging along for five hours, our spirits were down and we were hungry and tired. That's when the trek leader came up to me, put a hand on my shoulder and said, 'Ashdin, you see that blue-roofed hut?' pointing at a speck a few mountains away, 'that's where we lunch'. My heart sank. I wanted to shout every single swear word I knew. I was hungry and tired and wanted to just sit and chill.

When we are destination-oriented, we often feel like this. It just looks so impossibly far away. What is the point of taking that journey? It is just going to be hard and long and impossible. Sam sensing my anger smiled and said, 'Ash look around, see where you are! Breathe in the air! Then just take one step and then the next and then the next.'

So, I looked around took a sip of water and took a step forward. I just focused on the step I was taking at that moment. Soon that impossible distance had been covered and I found myself digging into a big plate of fried rice and hot soup.

Distance to the destination can scare us, but don't be in a hurry to reach it.

Instead, focus on one step at a time. Each step, in this story, is like a habit in our lives. Just focus on each step or each habit. Slowly, slowly, there is no rush. Spend time enjoying the view, enjoying the process. If you find enjoyment in the process, you will be unstoppable.

So as your Habit Coach, I say, 'who cares how long it takes to form a habit'. There is no destination. Let it take twenty-one days or twenty-one years. Each day you perform the habit you will grow. Find things to enjoy in the process and it will not be so hard, laborious and boring.

There's More to Habits

22

Can Bad Habits Be Good?

When I tell people that I am a Habit Coach the first thing they say is, 'Oh you should see all the bad habits I have'. or 'So you help people give up bad habits', or 'I only have bad habits; I don't have any good habits'. Funny how our minds are automatically tuned to our 'bad habits' and strange how many of us are slightly proud of our bad habits. Bad habits have this Bad Boy or Bad Girl enigma about them. A Bad Habit wears a leather jacket, sits in the corner of a shady bar smoking a cigarette, with a whisky on the rocks, and wears sunglasses at night. And of course, completely ignores you when you demand he leave. He puts up a real fight as you try to throw him out. What is it about bad boys, bad girls, and bad habits that make them so addictive, attractive and alluring? So, let's start by dismantling their charm.

Bad Habits Don't Exist!

Imagine if I told you that there is no such thing as a bad habit. Instead, it is playing an essential role in our life. The word 'bad' is a blanket statement. It means nothing. A white bread sandwich might be bad for a person with gluten intolerance, but is a saviour for someone starving to death. A job that I consider bad, might be a blessing for someone who has been unemployed for a year. I remember a friend of mine telling me she had run badly. She is an Iron Man athlete. And then she quoted an insanely quick time for running a marathon race. Now for me, her 'bad' time would have been my 'best' time!

Hence the word bad is misleading. What we normally call 'bad habits' are what society usually sees as 'bad habits'. We need to move away from calling them bad habits. So, my reaction, when someone tells me about how many bad habits they have is, 'There are no such things as bad habits. In fact, I never work with my clients on getting rid of their bad habits because those are irrelevant.'

The Journey of a Bad Habit: #Stage 1 – The Crutch

I like to think of a bad habit as a crutch. When someone has broken their leg and they need to walk, they use the support of crutches. That is the role of a bad habit. Most bad habits start off as compensation for an unfulfilled need. You might have started smoking because you wanted to hang with a group of friends but lacked the necessary social skills. You might have started drinking because your evenings were lonely and you needed company. You might laze in bed and hit snooze thirty-five times on your alarm because you detest your job.

All the things you consider bad habits now, were things that helped you at some point in your life. They weren't necessarily bad at the time. They were just taboo. If you are now at a stage in your life where you no longer require them, then you need to learn to let them go. This is the hard part. This is the stage when people trip up. This is what you need to learn.

So 'bad habits' start their life off as crutches to help you through a phase in your life, then they become so much a part of your life that it is difficult to let go of them. They turn into fluffy comfort blankets. (So much for the leather-wearing, biker dudes.)

A client of mine, the CEO and founder of a fantastic company, went through something similar. She had an absolutely brilliant mind and had achieved more success than anyone could have possibly imagined. However, every morning and evening she would smoke some weed. Now whether you believe smoking weed is a good habit or a bad habit, in this situation it is irrelevant. That is not the objective of this story. What's important is that she wanted to let go of this habit as she believed it was no longer serving her.

As always, I told her we will not get rid of it actively, but would focus on other areas of life. We started creating a very solid foundation of habits, things that nourished her mentally and physically. Gratitude exercises, meditation, sleep habits, exercise habits and nutrition habits.

One day we decided to understand the root cause of the smoking habit. It turned out that smoking was something she started in college. At a time when her marks were dropping and she was not doing too well. Weed was a crutch. It was easy for her to blame her drop in performance on the weed that she was smoking, 'It's because of that, I did not do well.' Later in life this made it easy for her to blame all the pitfalls of running her business on the weed as well. It was an easy scapegoat.

Every morning her first joint was a signal that her working day was about to begin. At the end of the day, when returning home, the joint was a sign that the working day had ended. It was a full stop to the stress of work and a start to life at home. This habit was clearly playing a role in her life. It would not be easy to let go of something so entrenched. As a result, we didn't try removing the habit till the foundation was set.

So, the CEO and I spent months just focusing on getting her foundation in place. An exercise routine, a gratitude practice, a reading and learning habit, a habit to spend time with loved ones, making sure she was eating clean and nutritious food and habits for her stress.

Once this foundation was strong, the need for the weed was removed. She didn't need it, she just smoked because it was that time of day to do it. Then all we did was identify a better habit to be done around the same time as she would smoke that weed. For example, her evening weed was replaced with exercise in the gym and a bath afterward. Her morning weed was replaced with a meditation practice. This transition took about three months and was so seamless that it removed the struggle from the process.

Now think about all your 'bad habits'. How many of them have stopped being a crutch and turned into comfort blankets. They have moved from things that served a purpose, to something that is just comfortable. This is also the stage when the 'bad habit' turns into your identity. You become a 'smoker'. You say 'I have a sweet tooth'. You say 'I am lazy', or 'I can drink more than anyone else'. You carry your bottle of alcohol on a trip somewhere, 'just in case' you can't find some there.

It is very difficult to detach yourself from your identity. Breaking an identity is like a mini-death. It is like losing a part of yourself, like an arm or a leg. This is why so many people stay in this phase. They are not strong enough to shed the identity.

As your Habit Coach, I want to show you how to become strong in other aspects of your life. Create a new identity, with habits that help you grow and add to your life. Only then should you work on shedding these 'bad habits', that are a part of your very thought identity.

The next stage of a 'bad habit' is when it becomes a comfortable part of our lives.

The Journey of a Bad Habit: #Stage 2—The Comfort Blanket

This is where the bad habit loses its edgy 'bad boy charm' and becomes a 'comfort blanket'—it is familiar, comforting, a part of our identity, *but serves no purpose.* At this stage the habit does not harm those around us to the point where we see them suffering. But we suffer at the very thought of having to stop! That's the grip it now has on us.

So when does a comfort blanket turn into an addiction?

A surefire way to assess this is to observe the effect our habit has on the people around us. Most 'bad habits' affect just our own lives. Once in a while if we smoke a cigarette out on the balcony or alone at home, it is just our lungs we are tarring with nicotine. If we have a drink every day it is just our liver we have to worry about. However if we *have* to:

- Smoke compulsively in the car with the kids in the back seat we are turning them into passive smokers, harming the health and development of their little respiratory tracts, and role-modelling smoking as a positive coping habit; which it is not. Our smoking is now an addiction; no longer a comfort blanket.

- Drink every night till we get drunk and can even get violent. We have to be taken care of by our suffering family. We are addicted to alcohol and are alcoholics; long past the comfort-blanket stage.
- Eat way too many sweets (even if we have diabetes and obesity). Our loved ones will suffer and will have to take care of us. This is an addiction, no longer a sweet comfort blanket.

So if we are indulging in a 'bad habit' that does not as yet affect our loved ones and is a comfort blanket, we need to make sure it does not evolve into an addiction.

The thing is, once any unhealthy habit evolves into a comfort blanket and once that comfort blanket begins to be frequently used we are on the brink of turning into an addict or already are one.

The Journey of a Bad Habit: #Stage 3—Addiction

There are many ways of defining and measuring addiction. Some measure a physiological response in our brain, the way pleasure neurotransmitters are released or not released. The way dopamine works in the case of addiction is fascinating—the 'dopamine high' takes place *before* (and not after or during) the addictive activity. Which means the dopamine high exists:

- *Just before* we light the cigarette.
- *Just before* we take that first sip of our drink.
- *Just before* we bite into that brownie.

The repeated quest to get that dopamine high—when the high lies largely in the anticipation of fulfilling this craving, regardless of consequences—is what I would describe as 'negative pleasure'. Let's look at how 'negative pleasure'-seeking can develop with us.

Negative pleasure: Most addictive behaviours start off as activities that give immense pleasure. Think about opening a cold beer on a warm day. Think about biting into that chocolate cake. Think about opening your favourite social media app, or better still biting into a nice ripe mango. That first bite is pure pleasure, joy, happiness all rolled into one. It transports you back to your childhood. You gobble up that mango as fast as you can. If pleasure was an object, it would be this first mango!

The second mango is cut. You take a bite and ah! that sweet flavour dances on your tongue. That little bit of sour lingers and adds to the playfulness of the fruit. But it is never as pleasurable as the first mango, have you noticed that? You now cut the third mango. And start eating it. It is okay. Still as yummy and flavourful. But the pleasure is slowly disappearing.

Economics calls this the Law of Diminishing Marginal Utility i.e., all else being equal, as consumption increases the marginal utility (in this case pleasure) derived from each additional unit (additional mangoes) declines. Normally, it would make sense to stop an activity once it stopped giving us pleasure, so we'd eat a few and then lose interest. But some of us do not and that's the crazy thing!

We continue an activity even after pleasure reaches zero. We carry on doing it even though we aren't enjoying it anymore. We can reach a point when we actually dislike it, but cannot stop and still want more. After the fifth mango, now feeling sick, physically and mentally, we carry on eating and have reached the eleventh....you get the drift?

We are upset with ourselves (so is our tummy), and the positive pleasure has now turned into a negative feeling.

Most addicts fall into this category. They find no pleasure in the activity. But they just can't stop. They will make bargains with themselves. They will tell themselves that they are fools and idiots. But will continue with the activity. This is why guilting an addict to change their ways does not work.

Addicts already know what is wrong and can't help themselves. They know it is bad, but can't stop. Worse, there is no joy or pleasure left in that activity, eventually they are just left feeling negative all day long with awful feelings (such as helplessness, self-pity, self-reproach) and in more serious instances (as with alcoholism and drug abuse) the loss of an increasing amount of self-esteem and faith in oneself. Temporary relief (aka pleasure) is gained by doing whatever one is addicted to.

All of this equals to Negative Pleasure (mild, moderate or extreme). Sounds like insanity, doesn't it? But we all have our mini and major addictions. Mine was chocolate. If I started with just one piece of chocolate, I would end up finishing the box. After the first five pieces, I'd be hating myself and still reaching for number six. It used to be terrible until I learned ways of dealing with it. When we are addicted to something we derive no pleasure from it, but just can't stop.

A few years ago, I went to a casino in London. It was one of the fanciest ones there. The opening bets were so high that there was no chance that I would play, so that saved me from any chance of getting hooked, but I walked around and observed the players. It was about 1:30 a.m. and all the amateurs and fun-seekers had left. What remained looked like ghostly corpses. Mechanically placing bets. No joy or upset when they won or lost. They just looked for their next bet. I stayed back for another hour and did not see a single person smile! It was scary, so I left. It was a world of Negative Pleasure. That is what addiction looks like.

Notice—are the people in your life just complaining about the habit, or are they suffering because of it? If they are suffering, the cool dude (aka the bad habit) in the leather jacket who once looked so enticing, is now nothing more than a 'useless bum' (aka an addiction) ruining other people's lives, and it is time you reached out for help.

In sum, the three stages of negative pleasure are: first 'the crutch', a compensatory behaviour that serves a useful purpose; second, when it has been in use long enough to become our 'comfort blanket'—a habit that is familiar, comforting and (a what should be a red flag for us) a part of our identity—but serves no purpose; third, when we are no longer in control, the habit is. The addiction is when the habit no longer gives pleasure, or even comfort, but scares us but we can't stop it.

Clearly, there is so much to a bad habit. It is not black and white. Especially since a bad habit at one point was helping us through life. It was an aid to our life. It was making up for deficiencies in other areas of our life. In other words, until it crossed into stage three (an addiction) it wasn't really all that bad.

A better way to think about bad habits overall is to identify them as '*habits that have stopped serving me*' (and this includes addictions!). These were habits that played a role in our life and served a purpose. But no longer.

Be compassionate, these bad habits were probably trying to protect us from something worse. You are lucky they were there for you when you needed them. For convenience, we will continue using the words 'bad habit'.

But now you know what 'bad habits' really are—*habits that have stopped serving me and you*!

Exercise

Take a hard look at your life. Now pass all the habits you can think of through a three-step filter.

1. *How is this habit trying to help me or serve me?*
2. *Is this habit needed for the person I want to become?*
3. *Does this habit continue to serve me or am I just holding on to it?*

If the habit no longer serves you or adds to who you need to become and you are, then it's time to let it go, and for you to grow!

23

Breaking-up with Habits That No Longer Serve You

A strong foundation is created by building strong habits. Habits that serve you physically, mentally, socially and financially. Once you set these base habits in place, search for habits that bring you happiness and joy. These habits together will build the foundation on which you, as a human being, can thrive.

Such a foundation usually removes the need for bad habits. When your feet and legs are strong, you don't require a crutch. You can easily throw away any crutches you have and dance. Such a foundation prevents future bad habits from forming as well. When you have a strong foundation, you don't need to compensate with a 'bad' habit. A strong foundation creates a stable life and you become a stable human being.

So see which aspects of your life are currently being shaken up or destroyed by a weak foundation. Without a strong foundation, you are creating a skyscraper on a foundation of sand. It's not going to stand for long. A weak foundation is revealed by habits such as the inability to focus on a task; feeling lethargic quite often; relying heavily on stimulants, etc. Hence, we form compensatory bad habits like eating sugary sweets all day. The sugary sweets fix these slumps of low energy and focus. When I was unhealthy, I too used to have a handful of sweets in my trouser pockets every single day. These were there because I had not worked on my strong foundation yet.

So, start by giving yourself a strong foundation.

Pro Tip: Add more good habits to flush out the 'bad' habits. I started having black coffee (no sugar) and green tea. Soon I developed a taste for it and this good habit has stuck. These replaced the sugary tea I used to drink many times a day. Keep adding to your foundation with good habits and you will see the bad habits fall away. This is because the more 'good habits' you add, the less need there is for the bad habits. There is no way for them to serve you.

Going Cold Turkey vs. Tapering Down

Did you know that the expression 'Going Cold Turkey' possibly came from the similarities between a drug addict giving up drugs and the skin of a dead cold turkey? When you give up opioids or addictive substances, the withdrawal symptoms can be very intense. Among other symptoms, the skin can turn pale and get a grayish tinge, pretty similar to a cold, skinned dead turkey.

There is a lot of debate around quitting something cold turkey. Some people have successfully gone cold turkey, while others just bounce back fast. My grandfather, who was a chain smoker, had cartons of cigarettes under his bed. One fine day, he decided to quit smoking and very successfully did so. But promptly got addicted to popping pills. The cartons of cigarettes were replaced by cartons of medicines. Going cold turkey means giving up the 'bad' habit all out. Not tapering it down slowly, until it vanishes from your life. A one shot, clean swipe. The bad habit is kicked out of your life.

However, 'tapering down' is an essential part of giving up a bad habit. Remember the bad habit still plays a role in your life. Just like a person recovering from a broken leg, you have to do your physiotherapy exercises, get stronger and then start using the crutch, until you need it lesser and lesser. The crutch here being the bad habit. Do not go cold turkey when giving up bad habits. Instead, follow the Three Golden Rules Reversed for stopping a habit, as explained in the next chapter. However, there are times when you should try going Cold Turkey: The operative word here is 'try'. Think about going cold turkey:

- As an experiment or as a way to stretch your comfort zone.
- Do this in the form of challenges.
- A three-week challenge or a thirty-day challenge.

Challenges are very important tools to giving up a bad habit. Why? Because you know the challenge is not permanent, not lifelong. There is a certain ease or comfort in that fact.

The challenge also teaches you how you will feel when that addictive behaviour is not in your life. The challenge period will show you where are the pitfalls, the points that pinch in your journey to removing your use of the habit. It will show you what are the routines that will need to be reworked when you eventually give up the bad habit.

I like to use challenges when any behaviour has reached the stage of addiction. Where the behaviour brings you no pleasure but you still continue. I also like to use challenges when what is being used, has an addictive quality to it—Nicotine, Sugar, Porn, Alcohol, Caffeine (don't kill me), etc.

We have an entire chapter dedicated to challenges in this book (Chapter 20). I am a big fan of using challenges to make a change in our life. Not a permanent change, but the start of a change. I will share more about my first 100-days 'no-sugar' challenge, in the next chapter. It was scary and very life-changing.

So don't try stopping a bad habit cold turkey, instead use the cold turkey method when taking on a three-week or a thirty-day challenge.

To stop the habit simply reverse each of the Three Golden Rules, which is what we explore in the next chapter.

24

Reversing the Three Golden Rules

So, we have established that a certain habit is no longer serving you, or is no longer good for you. Next, you have started working on building a strong foundation of other good habits. Now it is time to slowly give up the habit and stop it once and for all. How do you rid yourself of a habit?

Simple, by reversing the Three Golden Rules of habit change.

Make the Habit Horribly Hard

This reverses the first two Golden Rules at a go! The first rule encouraged you to crunch the desired habit it down into 'stupidly small' steps; and further making the habit 'extra easy' by removing all friction that would stop you from getting the habit done.

Now we make the unwanted habit as long-winded, complicated and hard as possible to do. We want to make it so horribly hard to do, that you wonder is it even worth doing it! So, what does this look like in the real world?

If you want to give up smoking, get rid of all the cigarettes that you have at home, in your bag, or in the car. Then get rid of all the lighters and ashtrays. Sure, you might smoke when you are out with friends, but make the habit as hard to do as possible. Pay twice the cost of a cigarette if you ask a friend for one.

If you want to give up drinking every evening at home, lock the alcohol cabinet and give the key to your neighbour. So, if you feel like having a drink, you have to go ask them for the key. Now don't give the key to that neighbour you invite home for a drink every week. Give it to that grumpy neighbour who doesn't want to be disturbed.

I know people who are trying to give up sugar but will keep chocolates and candy around their room. Saying 'this is to improve my willpower'. Don't do that, it is a losing battle.

When I was quitting sugar, I told everyone in the office about it and asked them to help me by not tempting or offering me anything with sugar. The harder you make the habit to do, the easier it is to stop it. Just keep adding the friction.

Never Do It Two Days in a Row

This is a reversal of the Third Golden Rule—'Never miss two days in a row'.

To stop a habit, make sure to keep missing two days in a row. The more you miss, the merrier. This way we turn the power of repetition on its head. If you want to stop a habit you have to break the consistency. You have to make sure that you give at least one day as a break between doing the habit. Two days off is even better.

One of my friends baked a batch of brownies for me. This was when I was in the process of stopping my habit of having something sweet after dinner. My first reaction was to devour the whole tray in one sitting. (Yes, I have done it multiple times in the past.) However, I made a schedule—one piece on Monday, then one on Wednesday, and then Friday. Saturday and Sunday, I would avoid them. I needed to do this because I had to stop the habit of having something sweet as a default after every meal.

Eventually, you can whittle the habit down to twice a week. Then once a week and then use it on occasions only. By breaking the pattern of repetition, you are able to let go of the habit. In the process, whatever you have chosen to use as a replacement for the habit becomes the new stronger habit.

Reset the Routine

If you want to stop a habit you have to stop the habits that you do just before and just after it. This is what we call a routine. Often the previous habit triggers the habit we want to stop. Hence, resetting the routine is an essential step in this process.

A friend of mine was trying to give up his drinking habit. Every night he would sit with two big bottles of beer and drink. It was affecting his life and the life of his family as well. It was clearly an addiction. His routine was to finish work, drive home, stop at the same alcohol shop along the way, pick up the beer and drink it at night. This was a set routine. Every day he would leave work, determined not to stop at the alcohol shop. He would grit his teeth in determination to 'not drink tonight'. But on auto-pilot, he would park outside the shop, go in and buy the beers. He didn't want to. It was as if he had no choice. This is the power and the horror of a routine. Your routines can make you and break you.

We made a small tweak to this routine; he now took a different route home, absent of alcohol shops. The first week was tough. But it helped him reduce the number of times he was drinking in a week. Similarly, if you eat a donut every day with your office friends at 5 p.m. and it has become a routine, figure out how you can change it. I set up meetings at 5 p.m. so that I was not tempted by the donut.

Recently, during the lockdown, since we were all stuck at home, I got into the habit of eating an early dinner and then vegetating in front of the TV. This was a new behaviour for me. Earlier I would be out meeting friends every evening. I had a very active social life. However, now life was spent just sitting at home and being socially isolated. I wanted to change this habit. So what I began to do was to eat dinner in my exercise clothes. Then after dinner, I would sit for twenty minutes, put on my shoes and head out for a one-hour walk.

This way I got some exercise in, I would get an hour to listen to podcasts or audiobooks and I was not sitting in front of the TV. I changed my routine to stop a habit. Similarly, figure out what aspects of your routine need to change so that they don't cue or set up the habit you want to stop.

Show Yourself Compassion: Slip-ups Are Expected

It is very easy to be hard on ourselves, especially when there is a habit that no longer serves us. We feel it is a waste and want to get it out of the system. This is why many of us take a very hardline approach to the process. We try and break it with grit and determination. However, that, as shown in previous chapters, is not a very practical approach (it mostly works well only with challenges). When it comes to habit change, we are trying not to use grit and determination. Instead, we need to start using the Three Golden Rules reversed.

In the process, there will be times when we slip up. We have our ups and downs. There will be days when we are upset and fall back on the habit. There will be days when we are tired and don't have the energy to resist anything. It is okay. It happens to the best of us.

By now you know my one true nemesis is sugar. As I write this chapter, I remember what happened just yesterday. It was a long tiring day. I had spent the week writing the book, was clocking in 2,000 words a day. Feeling on top of the world, I go and open the refrigerator. My mother left a tub of Belgian Chocolate ice cream in the freezer. I shut the door immediately.

Then slowly opened it again. 'I'll just take one spoon.' It was frozen solid. 'I'll take it with me to my room so it has a chance to melt, while I watch some TV.' The next thing I know, the tub is half over.

It happens to us all. Yes, even to me as your Habit Coach.

It took an effort to shut the box and put it back in the freezer. The first few bites were amazing. The last two made me feel like crap! But I still ate them.

I realized what had happened. I felt terrible for the first ten minutes. Then I said, 'Its, okay. Show compassion.' The last time I had eaten ice cream was probably a month or two ago.

I used to feel terribly guilty when I indulged like this in the past. It was this sickly feeling that took over me. Till one day my yoga teacher explained it to me. 'No point feeling guilty about the indulgence. Indulge and enjoy every bite.' That hit home. Because if I did not enjoy it and still continued to do it, it would have become an addiction. Enjoying it actually helps to let go.

Today, as I write this chapter. I know that there is only one thing to focus on. Making sure I do not eat the rest of the ice cream today. It is a habit that I want to stop hence I must not do it two days in a row. At the same time, I must not dwell on this slip-up. It happens. We are all just human after all.

The Last Nail in the Coffin for a Habit You Want to Stop

How do you know when a 'bad' habit has finally left you? The last nail in the coffin for a bad habit is when your identity changes. When you no longer think of yourself as a 'smoker'. When you stop calling yourself 'lazy', 'foodie', 'sugar addict', 'porn addict', etc.

Look at the words you choose for yourself. When they change, when the way you describe yourself changes, that's when you know the bad habit has left you forever. So, end your bad habits by changing your self-image. When you call yourself a non-smoker; you will do what non-smokers do.

The Real Difference between a Bad Habit and a Good Habit

A very interesting thing about most 'bad' habits is that they give you 'instant gratification'. The feeling of pleasure is immediate. As soon as the activity is done, pleasure is felt. The pain comes later.

- The tub of ice cream that I ate felt so good with a tinge of guilt while eating it. The tummy upset came later.
- The 35 tequila shots felt amazing and let me loose on the dance floor. The hangover and headache came later.
- The cigarettes felt so good while smoking them. The lung disease comes later.
- The slot machines in Las Vegas must have felt so good while playing them. The feeling of being broke came later.

Most bad habits will follow a similar pattern. Of giving pleasure now and pain later. It is a good way to identify bad habits. A friend of mine used to say 'a moment on the lips, a lifetime on the hips'.

Now most habits that we consider 'good' habits are all about discomfort first and the benefit later. These are about 'delayed gratification'. I joke with my friends that 'no sane person enjoys doing burpees or running'. It is not a pleasurable habit when you are doing it. However, when you see yourself getting stronger and your body aches disappear, that's when you know its helping. You are taking the pain upfront for a benefit later on.

Eating a salad instead of junk food is another way in which we delay gratification. It is not as satisfying or pleasurable now but will save you a lot of future pain in the form of medical bills and chronic disease. It removes the real pain of a miserable future giving you a comfortable life.

Keep asking yourself, is this going to give me pleasure or pain in the future? Is this habit going to help me, is it going to serve me in the future? Good habits are like the old Spartan warrior saying, 'The more you sweat in training, the less you bleed in battle.'

25

Busting Habit Myths

There are so many myths that need busting when it comes to habits. These are things people have picked up in their lives. Things people have told them or articles that they have themselves read in magazines.

These myths drive me bananas because some of them are so outrageous. Then there are myths that I believed so wholeheartedly at one point of time, till experience and wisdom prevailed. Myths are things we believe in, but have no bearing in reality or any truth to them.

Habits Make Life Boring

This is something I hear so often. 'I am a person who does not like structure, if you tell me to do this every day, I will rebel and not do it.' Yet they put on their underwear and outerwear every day. They have a bath and brush their teeth every day (hopefully). They eat every day.

It is not the daily repetition that makes a habit boring, it is the feeling of being trapped in something you don't want to do that makes life boring. As soon as what you are doing feels like a chore, you feel trapped and hence want to break free from the boredom.

As we have seen in this book, our days are filled with habits. Right from the way we put on our shoes and socks, to the way we drive to work. Our day is a stream of habits. Habits make up our life! Hence, it is not that habits make life boring, boring habits make life boring!

Want a fun life, make sure you like all the habits you do! Make them fun.

Can't Teach an Old Dog New Tricks

You can't teach an old dog new tricks, is a phrase I have heard since the time I was a kid! It was used by all the grown-ups as an excuse for the way they were.

There is absolutely no truth to this. You can learn and change habits at any time in your life. There is no age limit to learning and there is certainly no age limit to changing for the better. Another phrase used along with this is, 'At my age how does it matter, if I was younger, I would have done it.' This drives me mad because we are relying on something as stupid as the earth going around the sun a set number of times to tell us if we can or cannot change for the better. There is never a bad time to change for the better.

Remember the rule of Kaizen, small improvements are all that are needed to take place. Most people who believe in this myth or offer it as an excuse, do so because they are afraid to put in the effort. It does not seem worthwhile to them because they cannot visualize the benefit.

I remember talking to a sixty-eight-year-old client. We were discussing why he should start exercising. He believed that there was no point because he didn't need muscles to impress anyone. 'Which young girl am I trying to impress with working out and muscles?' This was why he did not feel the effort needed for exercise was worthy. I spent a lot of time with him explaining the role of exercise, finally asking him, 'Are you happy with the aches and pains in your body? The pain you get every time you stand up and sit down. Or the backaches every night?'

He looked at me confused and said, of course, he did not. That's when I explained to him that the role of exercise was to take away these pains of growing older. To at least make him feel younger from the lack of pain and not to impress the girls.

As soon as he understood the benefit and believed it was worthy of effort, he immediately jumped on the opportunity to make exercise a habit. The more he felt his body getting stronger, the more he wanted to continue. By sixty-nine, he clearly was an old dog doing new tricks.

Rewards Help in Forming Habits

Rewards are a great way to treat yourself for a job well done. However, I have never seen them being used well for forming habits. Most people reward themselves with the things that they should ideally be avoiding. For example, I have seen brownies and ice cream set as rewards for following an exercise routine.

In order for a reward to work, it has to be in line with the objective of the habit. For example, if you maintain your home workout routine for two months, you can buy a gym membership. However, the reward is often not enough of a reason for many to stick to their habit.

The reward is supposed to motivate, but if you set your intention and follow the Three Golden Rules of habit change, you will not require the need for a reward. Remember motivation sucks, it is not reliable as a tool to help you create a habit or reach your goals. Hence, I am not a fan of rewards.

At the other end, we have punishments for failing to stick to a habit. I have had people give themselves all sorts of punishments like 'donating Rs 500 for every cigarette smoked', or 'one extra hour of cardio for eating a cake'.

The human mind cannot feel a 'future punishment' as well as it can feel a 'current pleasure'. If I can derive pleasure from it now, that is okay, the punishment is future Ashdin's problem. Hence, punishments don't seem to work either. How many times have we disobeyed our teachers and parents, when they told us not to do something and then threatened us with a punishment! It's human nature.

Choosing the right punishment is so important as well. If you chose a punishment like one extra hour of cardio for eating a brownie, then you are creating a negative association with cardio and with exercise. That is not a good thing either.

Hence the concept of using rewards and punishment for creating new habits is not really practical.

Missing a Day Will Break the Habit

This myth was brought about by habit-tracking apps that gamified getting 'habit streaks', basically, how many days in a row can you do a particular habit for. The goal when counting these habit streaks is to make sure you do not miss a day. As a result, there is so much pressure on the person to do the habit every day. I have seen people add punishments for days they missed the habit.

These kinds of habit streaks are not something that you can do long-term. It is great if you think of them as challenges for a set number of days. However, if you want to create a habit for the rest of your life, using habit streaks are not a good idea. Instead, we have to show compassion to ourselves for the days when it will not be possible to do the habit, on days we are feeling low or very stressed. I have seen people having a terrible day and then forcing themselves to do a habit they had committed to. They were stressed to begin with and this habit had just increased their stress load.

As your Habit Coach, I would much rather you follow the Third Golden Rule of habit change—'Never miss two days in a row'. This allows you to show yourself compassion on days where a habit just might not be possible. Missing one day will not ruin the forming of a habit. But missing two days definitely will. So never miss two days in a row. This is the key to consistency.

All Successful People Share the Same Habits

This is one of the biggest myths out there. We believe that we can imitate the habits of successful people and in turn, we will achieve the same level of success.

There are many things wrong with this myth. The first is that most successful people have taken different routes to their success. Some wake up at 4 a.m. and work hard in the morning. Others sleep at 4 a.m. having worked hard through the night. As outsiders, we see the 4 a.m. and try to imitate it. Instead, we need to understand *why* they do what they do. In this example the *why* is 'getting focus time, without distractions'. We need to learn the why and find our own perfect time slot to work without distractions.

The most successful bodybuilders and athletes sleep twelve hours a day. Imagine if you imitated their habits blindly. You would be asleep half your life! They do this because their body needs that extreme recovery. Your body does not. They sacrifice their social life, family life, etc. for their sport.

Warren Buffet drinks Coca Cola every day. Imagine if you had to imitate this habit of his. Yes, there are things you must learn from successful people and what they do. However, not all successful people have the same habits. Hence, there is no one clear path to successful habits.

The trick is to learn about how successful people have lived their lives. Then pick and choose habits that align with your life. Things you can start incorporating using the Three Golden Rules of habit change. Start small, you do not have to be as extreme as the successful people, they have had years of practice to get to where they are. You are just starting your journey. Learn but create your own. Not everyone is the same.

Resolutions Are Habits

I used to be a big fan of New Year resolutions. I loved them. In the past, a good New-Year resolution helped me get back into reading books. However, the way we use New Year resolutions nowadays is more like wishful thinking than actually making a change in our lives.

I have met so many people who swear that this year is going to be different. They have a new calendar and they have written their resolutions on that calendar! This time they will make that change that they have been trying to make for the last five years. It is just wishful thinking. Most New Year resolutions fail by mid-February. By the time half the year is over, only a handful of people would have maintained their resolutions. The ones that did, figured out how to make it a habit that they can do consistently.

New Year resolutions are not the same thing as habits, saying that they are propagating a myth. If you do want to create New Year resolutions this time around, do it. But follow the three Golden Rules of habit change to turn them into habits. Without following these rules, you will just be wishing with no results.

26

Five Success Stories

In this chapter, I'll give you five success stories of my clients who were able to bring about a change in their life through the power of habits. The change relates to all the major areas that we struggle with in our day-to-day lives.

1. Vishal and Daily Mobility

'I used to be an athlete. Ashdin, I have won medals for my school in hockey and athletics. I used to be able to do twenty to thirty pull-ups. Now if I bend down to tie my shoelace, I don't know if my back will support me in getting up again. I am scared of going for walks or climbing up the stairs at home.'

Vishal was an industrialist. Over the last thirty years he had dedicated his entire life to work, leading to a very sedentary lifestyle. He spent his work day seated on his fancy ergonomically-designed chair. At the end of the work day he sat in his cushy Mercedes on his way home. At home, he would sit on one of those big recliner chairs with a massage function. And he slept on a mattress designed to give the best back support possible. And yet, with all the comforts in the world, he spent his days in pain.

It took me a while to explain to Vishal that the more he used things to make his life comfortable, the less he used his actual muscles. Hence, over a period of time his muscles had gotten weaker. The solution here was to slowly bring movement back into his life. Make his body strong again and to do this while maintaining his insane work schedule.

His first rule was that he did not have time for going to the gym. So whatever we did had to be in tune with his daily work schedule. His intention was to: 'Live pain-free so that I can live life to the fullest without being scared.'

I then spent time understanding how Vishal worked. His time in office was spent in different ways.

1. One-on-one non-private meetings
2. One-on-one private meetings
3. Group meetings
4. Email time
5. Thinking time
6. Phone time
7. Video calls

I then associated four different sitting/standing/walking activities with each of the kinds of work.

1. One-on-one non-private meetings: To be conducted while walking on the factory floor. This way Vishal got to

see and interact with everyone on the floor as well, while having the meeting.

2. One-on-one private meetings: To be conducted sitting in his office, as these were sensitive discussions.
3. Group meetings: To be conducted standing if they were less than fifteen minutes. If they were longer than that, then Vishal could adopt a hybrid sitting-and-standing approach.
4. Email time: To be spent standing at the desk, and he installed a new standing desk where he could stand and work on his computer.
5. Thinking time: To be spent sitting on the sofa in his room. A change of seat helps the body move in a different way
6. Phone time: To be spent walking around the office.
7. Video calls: To be taken while seated at his (normal, not standing) desk.

After the first day of these new habits, Vishal felt like he had done a mini workout that day. I told him not to strain himself, but to start the habits in a small and manageable way.

After two weeks of maintaining these habits, Vishal's personal assistant told me that she had never seen him this active and full of energy in the last fifteen years. We had made his personal assistant his accountability partner. So she would make sure he followed the habits.

After three weeks Vishal wanted to level-up his movement habits. So we got a physiotherapist to come before lunchtime and make him do some strengthening exercises. This we did three times a week. This really helped his pain. After a month-and-a-half, Vishal was finally pain-free. He felt as if he had got his life back.

2. Akanksha and Nutrition

'Look, I have tried all the different diets. I have read books on keto. I worked with a dietician for six months and I lost weight. It all comes back immediately when I stop the diet. I don't know what to do to change this kind of yo-yo behaviour. This weight is affecting my self-confidence, I am now pre-diabetic, with PCOS [polycystic ovary syndrome] and have a fatty liver. I don't know what else to do.'

Akanksha was just thirty-two. The first thing I told her was that her weight issues had nothing to do with her self-discipline or her ability in any way. I told her the problem was that she only knew one way to lose weight, which was through a diet. Now the problem with diets is that they are short-term focused. You are either on a diet or off a diet. You are either losing weight on a diet or putting it back on once you are off the diet. All diets are temporary. I told her what needed to change was her foundations around food. Her habits around food. These habits over time would become her normal way of living. It would not be temporary like a diet.

Habit 1. Intermittent fasting: After a long discussion we arrived at an intention for intermittent fasting. *Note: The intention was not about eating less or calorie restriction.* Her true intention behind intermittent fasting was, 'to not have hunger or food control my life or my mood'.

With this intention set, we started off the intermittent fasting habit for just twelve hours. Then each week we increased it by two hours. So by the end of week three, she was comfortably fasting for sixteen hours. She did not feel like she was starving herself or restricting herself in any way.

At the end of two months, fasting was just a way of life and she was so comfortable with it.

Habit 2. Cutting down her post-meal sweet: This was a big deal for Akanksha as she would eat a healthy lunch and then have a huge dessert afterwards. This was a habit she had inherited from her parents. At the dining table, a plate of dessert was always served after a meal.

The intention: 'Sweets are great, and I don't want to be forced to give them up later if I get diabetes.'

We started the habit by stopping the dessert at night after dinner. Her habit was to go and brush her teeth immediately after her dinner. This way she got the taste of something sweet in her mouth and was not tempted to eat dessert and hence brush a second time.

Over the course of two weeks (yes habits take time, so be patient) we started to transition to having dark chocolate for dessert at lunch. Every week we went to a darker percentage of chocolate, till she was having 90 per cent. After a while, she realized that she was not craving the sweet anymore. She would go days without eating chocolate. The dessert habit was finally broken.

Habit 3. Increasing vegetable and protein consumption: Most of us do not eat enough vegetables and proteins in our meals. Instead, we cover our plates with the carbohydrate of choice, either rice or roti or bread or potatoes. A very small portion of our plate is dedicated to vegetables and proteins. Interestingly, most of the nutrition our body needs resides in vegetables and proteins. Proteins are the building blocks of our body, so we need a good amount of protein for a healthy body. Vegetables give us vitamins and minerals. Both of these also take longer to digest and make us feel fuller longer.

Intention: 'I want to give my body the nutrients it needs.'

So the habit we created was to divide the plate into quarters. Twenty-five per cent of the plate had to be filled with protein. Fifty per cent of the plate had to be filled with vegetables (potatoes do not count). Twenty-five per cent of the plate had to be filled with the carbohydrate of choice.

This made her food choices easier. She could no longer just eat a risotto or a pizza for a meal and be done with it; this would violate the plating rule. She had to start thinking about her meals. This changed her relationship with food. She was now seeing it as the raw material of her body, instead of something one ate for taste alone. In the first month, Akanksha dropped 6 kilos. And kept losing weight the months after. After six months her test results showed a big difference in her fatty liver and her pre-diabetic condition.

My favourite moment is when I got a picture from her buying a new set of clothes because her old clothes no longer fit her.

3. Shivani and Sleep

'Ashdin, there is no way I get to sleep before 1:30 at night. My mind is racing and all sorts of thoughts keep coming. I try and watch the news or pour myself a drink to drown it out. But I keep getting such disturbed sleep. Then in the morning, I am so tired that I wake up at 9 a.m. and cannot give my full 100 per cent at work. I have tried setting the alarm for 5 a.m. to wake up, but I just can't. I am frustrated and don't know what to do.'

This was the brief given to me by Shivani. She was the CEO of a very big company. And for many years her sleep cycles had gone for a complete toss. She could not figure out what to do about them. She had noticed that her work was suffering as well in the process. She used to be a morning person, would wake up and exercise early. But with this new sleep schedule, all of that had stopped. She wanted to wake up early and enjoy the day.

After talking to her. We settled on her intention for sleeping early and waking up early. It was: 'I want to feel like I have maximized and not wasted my day'. This is such a powerful intention. Note we created an intention for her entire night routine and not just for one habit.

Then I explained to Shivani that the morning routine starts the night before. If you want to have a great morning, you first have to have a solid night routine. I added only three small habits to her nightly routine. We first established a cue. At midnight, an alarm would ring and this alarm was set to remind her it was time for sleep. Once it rang she had to do the following.

Habit 1. Turn off or dim all the lights to a bare minimum. And switch off screens: She needed to do this because bright lights trick the body into thinking that it is daytime. Our lights at home are so bright that our body thinks of them as sunlight. The same thing happens when we are constantly on our screens. The blue light from the screens makes us feel like it's midday. In this way, our main sleep hormone melatonin is disrupted. Thus keeping us awake, instead of making us feel sleepy.

Habit 2. Journal the activities of the day in her book: This habit was done so that she could calm her mind down before going to bed. All the thoughts of the day would now be out on paper and she could relax. Very often the endless thoughts we get when trying to sleep are nothing but all the things we have been ignoring or running away from throughout the day. When you journal them down, it is as if we have listened to them and they will no longer run amock in our minds.

Habit 3. Listen to an audiobook or a podcast instead of the news: The news is often negative information. It is not what we want to be filling our mind with before going to sleep. The same goes for watching shows. We believe that our eyes need to be tired in order to sleep. Which is why we try watching TV or some screen before bed. The truth is that the mind and eyes need less stimulation in order to sleep well. When you listen to an audio book or a podcast the mind automatically slows down. It is not as stimulated as visual stimulation.

Pro tip: Listen to a podcast or audio book at .75x speed. This way the person talks even slower and hence makes the mind settle down to sleep.

Shivani added these habits to her routine. And every week we set her bedtime half-an-hour earlier. We also made her wake up half-an-hour earlier. In this way she was slowly moving towards her ideal time. Shivani now wakes up at 5 a.m. and has a very solid morning routine along with the habit that she incorporated into her evening routine.

4. Meeta and Feeling Stuck

'I don't know what has happened to me. I just don't feel like doing anything. Every morning I wake up and think that today I will go for a run or today I will work on my business or today I will eat healthily. Then I just sit and binge-watch different serials on Netflix. I eat all the junk food possible, while watching. I don't know what to do. I am so demotivated.'

Meeta was a high-powered working professional, who had recently quit her job to work on her start-up. For the last few months, she had been in this funk. She felt stuck in this cycle of waking up and not being productive. She had gotten into this habit of starting her Netflix shows while having breakfast in the morning and she continued to watch them all through the day.

After spending time talking to her about the things she enjoyed doing I realized that she loved going for a run. So I decided to make the morning run her anchoring habit.

An anchoring habit is a habit that holds the routine and the rest of the day in place. Very often when our days seem to just float around, it is because we do not have a strong anchoring habit.

Habit 1. Morning Run: Meeta's intention: 'I feel like I have achieved something and it gives me energy for the rest of the day.' To begin with, the habit was just to change her clothes and put on her running shoes. I wanted to get Meeta to stop sitting in front of the TV as her morning routine. This way she got a chance to get out of the house and hence, she would not turn on her TV.

Meeta had full reign over running or walking on any particular day. I made her listen to *The Habit Coach* podcast while running so that her mind was filled with positive ideas. Meeta noticed on days she ran, the rest of her day was much better. This kept fuelling her desire not to miss a day of this habit.

Habit 2. Scheduling: Meeta's intention: 'I don't want to waste a moment of the day, each moment is precious'. Once she sat down for work, Meeta ended up spending all her time in front of a laptop screen. She felt overwhelmed by other undone tasks and did not know where to start.

So the habit we created was for Meeta to sit down and plan just three tasks she had to complete that day for work. Just three tasks that had to be done. This was such a radical departure from the way she used to work. Her daily to-do list had at least forty things on it. She would feel so overwhelmed seeing that list that she would end up doing nothing.

What made this habit really powerful, was that she planned her day after she came back from the run. Hence she would be filled with endorphins making her feel good while making that long list! Now the goal of just three tasks took that overwhelming load away.

Habit 3. Stop episodes mid-way: Meeta said 'Binging makes me feel tired and lethargic', she realized that after binge-watching the shows she would actually feel physically tired. Often, while binge-watching, we have no control or count on the number of episodes we have seen. These shows have been designed to be exciting and leave you at a cliffhanger moment. When something new and dramatic is revealed, you want to go and watch the next episode.

Meeta's intention was to stop this binge-watching habit. The trick to stopping binge-watching is to realize that the middle part of the episode is normally a little boring. The story slows down. This is the time to stop and switch off the show. Then you can continue watching it the next day. So the habit is to stop an episode when you catch yourself being distracted. If you realize you aren't paying attention to what is going on, just switch the TV off.

Meeta set an evening TV time for herself and began implementing this habit of stopping the show at the slow moments. This way she would only watch about two episodes. Half the episode of the previous day (the ending), a full new episode and then half of another episode. Two halves and one full episode.

Meeta's life started to change. She felt physically fitter and her junk food habit decreased. She was getting more work done than she had earlier on. And most importantly, she was not wasting her time in front of the TV anymore.

5. Nimit and Anxiety

'Ashdin, there are days when I am so stressed that I cannot even function. I feel like the whole world is out to get me. Like there is no peace in my mind at all. I am constantly worrying about the future. Sometimes I feel it is difficult to breathe and the weight of the whole world is on my shoulders.'

Nimit used to work in a multinational company. He was on his way to the C-suite, worked very hard and was growing fast in the company. He had always been this kind of a Type A person. Believed in the hustle. After speaking to Nimit, I realized that there were three things he had to work on. The first was some way to get out of his fear. The second was to calm his stress response. The third was some way to get quiet time.

Habit 1. Gratitude practice: Nimit's stated intention was: 'I want to acknowledge all the wonderful things in my life and not feel entitled'. Gratitude is such a powerful tool for the mind to start relaxing. The mind cannot hold gratitude and fear at the same time. Since Nimit was constantly in a state of fear and worry, gratitude was a great place to start. This habit would help him get over some of the irrational thoughts and fears that he was having.

We linked the gratitude practice with Nimit's morning cup of coffee. He would write down three things he was grateful for in his journal. It was essential that he wrote the full sentence each time 'I am grateful for…' Soon he realized just how many wonderful things were happening to him. He was not being reactive and the fears he was holding on to, started disappearing.

Habit 2. Breathing: We don't realize this but when we are stressed, our breathing changes. We start breathing from our chest and take shallow breaths. Or worse, we hold our breath altogether. One day when I was with Nimit, he received a mail from his boss. At that moment, while his email was loading, Nimit stopped breathing. He was holding his breath in anticipation of what was to come next. It is very important to keep breathing as we move to potentially stressful situations. So, I taught Nimit the basics of breathing.

Every morning before getting out of bed, he would lie down on his back, place his right hand on his stomach and left hand on his chest. He then had to breathe in and push his belly out. And then when he would breathe out he had to pull his belly in. This is the correct way of breathing in a stress-free environment. Notice puppies and babies. They all breathe like this.

Next, I told Nimit to be aware of how he would breathe in meetings and to practice belly breathing during the meeting. Soon he noticed himself calming down in the most stressful situations. All by focusing on his breath.

Habit 3. A long walk: I noticed that Nimit had settled into a routine where he was either working or lazing, or watching TV—trying to numb his mind. So we added a post-dinner walk to his routine. The idea of the walk was to give him free time to process the things that happened that day.

When we sit and watch TV, we think we are relaxing. But actually, we are just distracting ourselves from what is important. When we go for a walk, we allow our minds to think and process. This helps us to complete thoughts that might otherwise have caused us stress. The habit was to walk without a podcast or music or any distraction. Just him walking with his thoughts for thirty minutes.

After a week of practising this habit, Nimit told me that he no longer felt the weight of the world on his shoulders. This is because he had given his mind enough space to deal with all the stressful thoughts that were running around in his head. As a result he felt free and light again.

Conclusion

Living Your Awesome Life

I have lived many lives. The name has stayed the same. The person has changed.

I am no longer the child I used to be. I am no longer the loner in school. I am no longer the geeky boy in college. I am no longer the man hungry for money and success. I am no longer the same person I was just a year ago. In the same way, look at your life. Notice how you have changed over the years. There is no way you are the same person you were fifteen years ago. Your thinking would have changed, your body would have changed and your life would have changed.

Speaking of change, there is a theory that every seven years, all the cells in your body are regenerated. So, even the matter that forms your body is not the same in seven years. I found this fact fascinating and I thought to myself. Imagine if I can give my body the best possible raw materials and the right kind of habits so that in seven years I would have a new awesome body! Wouldn't that be magical?

Keeping this thought in mind, I started changing my life. The quality of the ingredients in my food changed. The kind of exercise I did changed. I focused on my hormones and the way they were used in my body. I focused on my breathing and the way I used it to calm down or get healthier. Along with taking care of the physical body, I started focusing on my mind. Observing the thoughts and feelings I had. Learning how to change them, or tweak them.

Our thoughts are powerful things that have the ability to shape our lives and our future. Our thoughts are also part of our daily habits. You are reading this book because you want to make a change in your life and improve it for the better. You want to grow and make your life awesome. Who wants a normal mediocre life anyway? We want ours to be awesome!

In order to have that awesome life, you have to become the kind of person that can have an awesome life. As your Habit Coach, I have shown you how you can become the person you have always wanted to be, by following the simple steps that I've shared in the book. So far, most of your daily habits were created subconsciously. By creating a strong intention and then following the Three Golden Rules of habit change, you are creating habits consciously. Living life consciously.

Reading this book is just the first step on your journey to an awesome life. The real work starts now. As you close this book and read this last line, take three deep breaths and take your first step towards your awesome life.

I am Ashdin Doctor, your Habit Coach, and remember Awesome Lives Start with Awesome Habits.

Acknowledgements

Writing this book was the easy part. But making it awesome was possible because of the awesome team. Thank you, HarperCollins India, for betting on this new author and publishing this book. Cheers to many more!

Firstly, I want to thank the amazing HarperCollins India team. Ridhima Kumar, who patiently guided me through the publishing process. Who must have read the book more times than I can count to structure it well. We have a shared goal to see a sticker on this book that says, 'Over 1 million copies sold!' (Dear reader, help us reach this goal)

Next, I want to thank Sashii Ayer, the editor on this book, who worked on the story flow and language to get my points across to you, the reader.

Then the design team who worked on the cover and made it look attractive and energetic. Thank you, Ramnika Sehrawat and Amit Malhotra.

I also want to thank Tara Khandelwal at Bound India who coached me while I was still writing this book, before I got in touch with the publishers. Her insights like, 'Ashdin, this book is on habits and you haven't said the word "habit" once in the opening chapter!' were 'aha moments' for me.

I also want to acknowledge the role of Covid-19 pandemic that has been instrumental in giving me time and space for writing this book. On the one hand, it messed up with our daily working habits, but on the other hand it gave us new habits that are necessary to achieve new things.

This book wouldn't have been possible without the power of universe and serendipity. It was in 2021 when I went to Soho House in Mumbai to meet a friend for breakfast. There, I bumped into Kubbra Sait, another friend, who was sitting with her editor from HarperCollins India. The editor looked at me and asked, 'Aren't you that Habit Doctor?' I corrected her saying, 'Yes, the habit coach.' To my surprise she then said, 'We have been wanting to reach out to you for a book. Will you write one?' With a huge smile on my face, I replied, 'It's already written. When can we publish it?' :) (I had already finished writing the book two weeks back and was planning to self-publish it) This is the way the universe works. When you are ready, everything falls into place. Luck is just preparation + opportunity.

Finally, I want to acknowledge you—my reader. This book is a labour of love by me and the entire team part of the process. Enjoy it, finish it, use it and please share it with your friends and family. Be a part of this amazing journey. If we all start living awesome lives, we will have an awesome world!

Notes

Introduction

1. Duhigg, Charles (2012). *The Power of Habit: Why We Do What We Do, and How to Change*. Random House Trade Paperbacks.
2. Clear, James (2018). *Atomic Habits: Tiny Changes, Remarkable Results*. Avery.

3. Habits Are Hereditary

1. [US] National Science Foundation, News Release (3 February 2011): The Most Genes in an Animal? Tiny Crustacean Holds the Record'. https://www.nsf.gov/news/news_summ.jsp?cntn_id=118530#:~:text=Scientists%20have%20discovered%20that%20the,to%20have%20its%20genome%20sequenced.
2. Here are three articles that shed light on this interesting new area of study:
   (i) Centres for Disease Control and Prevention (n.d.) 'What is Epigenetics?' https://www.cdc.gov/genomics/disease/

epigenetics.htm#:~:text=Epigenetics%20is%20the%20study%20of,body%20reads%20a%20DNA%20sequence

(ii) Ling, C. and Ronn T. (2019), 'Epigenetics in Human Obesity and Type 2 Diabetes', *Cell Metabolism* 7 May, 29(5): 1026–44. https://www.ncbi.nlm.nih.gov/pmc/articles/PMC6509280/#

(iii) Haluskova, J. (2010), 'Epigenetic studies in human diseases', Folia Biol (Praha), 56(3): 83–96. https://pubmed.ncbi.nlm.nih.gov/20653993/#:~:text=The%20studies%20of%20epigenetic%20mechanisms,as%20for%20progressive%20pharmacological%20treatment.

10. Golden Rule #2: Make It Extra Easy

1. Little, J. and McGGuff, D. (2009), *Body By Science: A Research Based Program for Strength Training, Body Building, and Complete Fitness in 12 Minutes*. New York: McGraw Hill.

21. Habits Are Not about the Goal Alone, Habits Are about the Journey

1. Maltz, M. (1960). *Psycho Cybernetics: A New Way to Get More Living Out of Life*. New York: Simon and Schuster.

About the Author

Ashdin Doctor is The Habit Coach™ who believes that 'Awesome Lives Start with Awesome Habits'. He is the founder of Awesome 180 (www.awesome180.com), a habit coaching programme. He also hosts a popular podcast, *The Habit Coach with Ashdin Doctor*, which has over 900 episodes and has been featured in the lists of many top self-development podcasts in India.

Based out of Mumbai, Ashdin has been transforming the lives of many through his one-on-one habit coaching sessions. Drawing on his years of experience as a habit coach and after experimenting with different habit formation techniques, Ashdin offers practical and simple steps for personal change in this book.

Ashdin is also the director at Ormax Consultants Private Limited, Ormax Media Private Limited and Ormax Evolve Private Limited. He is also a trustee at Light of Life Trust—an NGO dedicated to the welfare and education of underprivileged children around the world. A percentage of the proceeds from this book will be donated to the NGO.